EFFECTIVE PR
MADE EASY

LAWPACK

About the author

Ian Proud's career in PR has spanned over 30 years. His first job was at Thomson Regional Newspapers where he started as a commercial graduate trainee. He left there to go to the Government Information Service where he worked in two busy Government departments, Defence and the Northern Ireland Office. After 15 years, the attractions of commercial PR beckoned and since then he has had various roles in this sector, from media relations executive responsible for PR for the defence electronics division at Plessey Company plc to head of corporate affairs for Ocean Group plc and Seeboard plc. He presently works as a freelance consultant and advises and implements corporate communications programmes for a wide range of companies and organisations.

In addition, Ian was a member of the Territorial Army as Royal Engineers Major for many years. Whilst there, he worked in the Media Operations Group (Volunteers) as the training officer responsible for the military and professional PR training of the unit's officers.

Effective PR Made Easy
by Ian Proud

© 2002 Law Pack Publishing Limited
Photographs © Ian Proud
Cartoons © John Rush

LAWPACK

76-89 Alscot Road
London SE1 3AW
www.lawpack.co.uk
All rights reserved.

ISBN 1 902646 96 7

Note: In this book, for 'he' read 'he or she'.

Table of contents

# Introduction

> 'Public relations is planned, sustained communication between an organisation and its target audiences' - **The Institute of Public Relations**

The definition of PR appears to be deceptively simple. What makes it difficult is that the aim of PR is to gain a pre-determined and desired reaction from the target audiences. A journalist aims to gain a reaction from the reader, typically of, 'Oh! How terrible!' 'Oh! How interesting!' 'Oh! How fascinating!'

PR seeks to gain a positive reaction for the company or organisation: 'How profitable!' 'How innovative!' 'What good management'. Reactions like these help to ensure that companies and organisations gain and hold a good reputation amongst their target audiences. With a good reputation achieved and maintained, such bodies can improve sales, recruit more easily, introduce new policies and generally build on their success.

Such a deceptively simple definition, along with the benefits of a good planned PR programme, can only be achieved by careful integration of all the means of communication available. Most importantly, the full commitment and support of senior managers is absolutely vital.

Those actually responsible for PR are the Chief Executives, regional directors and country managers, etc. All these are people in responsibility with whom the buck stops when it comes to PR. Experienced managers also now find that they have to be competent spokesmen as well. Businessmen concerned about the ill-informed environment in which they operate will also find this book of use. In many cases, businessmen and senior managers can, and should, call on professional support to ensure they communicate properly and accurately. This book will not only be of use to PR professionals, but it will also be invaluable to businessmen and senior managers as it will not only provide them with guidance on managing PR, but they will also be better able to work with their PR advisers, be they in-house or external.

Using the advice, hints and procedures in this book, managers in business and other organisations will be helping to create a climate in which their organisation and business in general can prosper and succeed. For the PR practitioner, this book will provide the extra polish for the delivery of a successful service and for the manager, explanations on how misunderstandings occur and how to reconcile them.

Chapter 1
The value of communication

What you'll find in this chapter:

➡ The need for communication
➡ Sources of news

There is always a need to communicate. Many people who do so invariably know their subject outstandingly well as they will have worked their way up in their profession or business and will be able to speak informatively about it. What they also have to know is how to communicate effectively.

Over the last 30 years journalists have become more and more used to organisations making personnel available to speak to the press. It is difficult to identify a defining moment, but most likely it occurred when the Army went to Northern Ireland to support the Police in 1969. This was a journalist's dream environment, with plenty of dramatic action and people and politicians across the Province only too willing to speak. The resultant copy and footage grabbed the public's attention. Not to be outdone, the Army introduced a deliberate policy of allowing soldiers of all ranks to speak to the press. On most occasions a PR officer was present, but often Tommy Atkins was doorstepped on the streets. The result was always the same: a confident soldier knowing what he was doing, prepared to reply to press enquiries confidently, speaking simply and without saying too much. In total, it helped immeasurably to give the Army a favourable image.

But what is the value of communications? Quite simply the public expects it. If you are in the public eye, then you exist. If you do not have your views, opinions or news in the press or on the airways, then you are invisible, unknown; or even worse, you are perceived to have something to hide.

These are the facts of life in today's information-led world. The prickliest problem for any organisation is how to ensure favourable treatment from the media. Opposing them in achieving this aim are two misconceptions. Firstly, is the media's apparent intention of reporting bad news and, secondly, the seemingly off-hand manner the media treats the business sector in particular as a matter of course. Even if you do end up in front of a camera or a journalist's notepad, he ends up using a quotation out of context or a carefully planned interview is binned at the very last minute, or worse, parts of the interview might even be made up.

The bad news for those who want to communicate using the media is that bad news is always with us. Reporters and news editors want good stories, which is why disaster stories always sell newspapers and attract viewers. If it is not a disaster, the reporters are always looking for their own news angle, so it is up to companies and organisations to find their own with which to grab the attention of journalists.

A little initiative goes a long way. When I worked for Plessey, I ran a well attended press conference trailing the black boxes of electronics that would be shown at an exhibition in three months' time. After the presentation, I made sure that each journalist had a detailed briefing on a specific piece of equipment from the specialist concerned. In doing so, I made sure each journalist had his own story from the press conference and as a result the company had a large number of the electronic systems reported in considerable detail. The benefit of this is not only the press coverage, but we also gained the reputation for being very co-operative with the press.

So perhaps you have decided on a policy of positive communication with all your target audiences. Each of those audiences must be treated in the specific manner that will attract the favourable reaction, be it an organisation's employees, suppliers, clients, potential clients, shareholders, partners, etc. It seems obvious, but treating them all the same will be a glorious waste of time. Employees need different information from shareholders as do clients and suppliers. Not only does the information need to be tailored, but so does the means of delivery.

This book looks at what you can do to produce effective communication, minimise problems and even has some useful hints on how to complain effectively. But there are two lessons for those in the PR loop:

- A bad media encounter must not be taken personally. There are lessons to be learned, so you can turn them to your advantage later.

- Plan any media interview carefully. Identify your main two or three points carefully; say them succinctly and memorably so they can be put over concisely in a couple of sentences.

The first thermal imaging camera that did not need an integral cooling system. A Plessey executive holds the innovative piece of technology that made it happen with a thermal image on the screen beside him. The picture virtually says it all.

Sources of news

News is often defined as information which people do not want to be made public. Bad news may well be universal, but the United Kingdom is unique in the incredible variety of media outlets: probably thousands in number of newspapers, magazines, radio stations and TV stations combined. Then there is the countless number of news sources on the Internet.

Experience shows that the majority of people gain their news and knowledge of current affairs from television programmes. Surveys show that TV is good at giving impressions, whereas newspapers and other print media, with the advantage of being able to be read and reread, are better at transmitting ideas and other details.

Britain is a news-hungry country. More than 20 million people watch the evening news on the BBC, ITN and Channel Four, the combined circulation of the national daily newspapers is about 15 million, and each newspaper is read on average by three people; that is a readership of 45 million. Radio news and current affairs attract smaller audiences, but Radio 4's morning *Today* programme attracts a highly influential audience comprising the country's opinion and its news coverage often sets the agenda for the rest of the day's news. No other programme has Cabinet Ministers listening as a matter of course, but also takes calls from Prime Ministers correcting or updating its news reports.

The impact of appearing on any of these media means that one will be seen or heard by millions. One appearance may give a tremendous boost to the ego, but sustained communication is needed to ensure your messages are successfully transmitted. The PR practitioner must therefore tailor his approach to suit the needs of each of the media.

Chapter 2
News

What you'll find in this chapter:

➠ The media
➠ News appeal - the human angle
➠ Giving your story eye appeal
➠ Press briefing conventions

News is jokingly defined as something that someone somewhere does not want published. News is also what sells newspapers and attracts audiences to TV and radio stations. News is now; if it happened yesterday, it is history. But if a journalist finds a story that happened some time in the past and no one else has covered it, then that journalist will report it quite rightly as news, because it was unreported. Often a major story will be superseded by an even more important one, and if you have been involved in successfully persuading a reporter to carry your story, be prepared to see it spiked or swept onto the cutting room floor as the big story carries all before it.

In June 1989, I had successfully persuaded a radio journalist to produce a three-minute report on one of Plessey's electronic systems. The night before, I double-checked that the BBC Radio 4 *Today* producer had the tape ready for the next morning. I had the media monitoring agency tasked to record the programme, the Plessey managers were duly informed and the next morning I was up bright and early to hear my exquisitely planned report on *Today*. Unfortunately, other matters of importance were happening in the world at that time, it was the Chinese students demonstrating in Tiananmen Square, and for three hours I sat and waited just in case my report made the airwaves. Surprisingly it did not, but fortunately, most of the Plessey managers were aware that news editors prioritise news and that the events unfolding in China overwhelmed news of even the cleverest black boxes.

The first lesson of PR is that media relations is not an exact science. Yes, one can use experience and even contacts to maximise the chance of successful coverage; but sometimes news editors have stories that will be more appealing to their viewers and readers than your carefully crafted offering.

The media

To most people, the media comprises the electronic and print media. However, in the PR context, the media includes any means of communicating, internally or externally, with your target audiences. So this includes the Internet, intranets, brochures, in-house newspapers and even mailshots. All of them, with varying degrees of accuracy, are conduits for transmitting information. At one end of the scale, a personal letter ensures that your recipient reads your message, while at the other end, an interview on the BBC World Service will be heard by an audience of approximately 140 million people. All media can be used to carry your messages with varying degrees of intensity and accuracy.

When using the media, you want the audience to respond positively to you. An advert in the print media is fine for advertising a service or product to sell. You might be sufficiently sophisticated to run corporate image adverts, but the readers and viewers know that the adverts carry what you want to say. Any attempt to attract favourable attention using adverts is likely to attract the famous Mandy Rice-Davies retort, 'Well, he would say that, wouldn't he?'

If you want the readers' positive response, your news has to be in the news columns. Nothing succeeds as well as having your news reported by a respected, third-party reporter. Readers and viewers will trust his journalistic judgement, whether it's in a national newspaper or an erudite trade magazine. So if this is the route to success, how do you make contact with this magical being? How do you gain his attention? How do you persuade him to write so glowingly about you and your organisation?

The answers to these questions are in the way you respond to his questions:

- How do I fill the columns this week?

- Is it news?

- Will I receive it well before the deadline?

- Is the boss available for interviews or questions?

If the news media is to be one of your main lines of communication with your target audiences, then you must know the mind of a journalist. The first priority of every news editor and the team of journalists is to fill the columns or programme time and ensure it hits the streets at a time when people will buy it, watch it or listen to it. They are rather like you and your organisation with targets to achieve and profits to be delivered. So with the media's insatiable demand for copy, there should be every good chance that you could be in the news.

Despite the faults that some associate with journalists, such as lack of accuracy, bias, cunning, cynicism and scepticism, do not forget that what you read over the breakfast table or on the journey home at the end of the day is put together by people whose aim in life is to gain a reaction to something that is stunning, cruel, clever, emotional or interesting. You may find it informative and possibly entertaining, yet it has all been written by a journalist, the type of person you feel you ought to distrust.

Putting the boot on the other foot, what does the journalist think about his local traders and businessmen? Someone too busy to talk to the press, perhaps introverted and secretive, and therefore very likely to have something to hide?

So both sides have more than a hint of mutual distrust and an air of confidence. The journalist knows he is doing his reporting well, because people continue to buy his magazine or newspaper in good quantities or there is a large number of viewers or listeners to the electronic press. The businessman, on the other hand, knows he is successful because his company is doing well with healthy sales, reasonable profits and the workforce is reasonably secure. Overall, he is contributing positively to the local economy.

Despite what people think, the journalist on the average national or regional daily is a highly experienced writer. Climbing the career ladder normally means starting on the local weekly newspaper, covering weddings, funerals, local council meetings, planning disputes and keeping in touch with the local police station, ambulance station, hospital, sports clubs, etc - all the local sources of news that people in the circulation area want to read. Much of what they write may well be of interest to the national newspapers and their stories are offered to them, and as one builds a reputation, the chances for advancement to a national newspaper beckon.

If you look carefully at your national newspaper, you will find that probably two-thirds of the news stories come from local news agencies, freelance reporters and local reporters. The paper's own reporters are responsible for the minority of the news stories. In order to produce a newspaper that will appeal everyday to their readers, news editors have to fill the paper with interesting news stories, features and, to make money, adverts. Many of you will have your own favourite writer or reporter whose items you will initially look for because you like their style or the authority with which the subject is covered. It is likely that any story covered by a respected journalist will be of extra interest to you and you will have quite a strong and positive reaction to that particular report. You will also notice that the journalist has reported the news accurately and, to show no bias, he will have taken the trouble to balance the story with comments from the other side of the fence. This search for balance is most obviously seen in the coverage of politics: a quotation or report on a political party's activities is almost always balanced by a quotation from the opposite party; so the reader can be aware of both points of view and the reporter can be seen to be unbiased.

If you have noticed this, then when you use the media as a conduit of information to your target audiences, you are most of the way to knowing the basics of media relations. To gain a positive reaction from the readership or viewers, try for respected third-party reportage of your activities. Make sure that the facts you give the journalist are accurate, unambiguous and newsworthy. Ensure that the story you give the journalist is sufficiently robust to withstand any critical comment that may arise from the balancing comment. If you do all of this and maintain good relations with your 'friendly' journalists by providing them with a constant supply of news, then you may find yourself being contacted as an 'industry' source and being asked for your comments in order to balance a reporter's news report.

For many businessmen, the balancing comment can completely ruin a carefully presented news story and can be cause for dissent with the media. But on the other hand, when confronted with the opportunity for a balancing comment, what would you do?

Many years ago, Edinburgh Airport was to be enlarged and there was a great deal of opposition to the proposal. A journalist on *The Scotsman* noted all the comments from the groups opposed to the runway extension. To balance the story, the journalist decided to contact the Army press desk at the Ministry of Defence for comment, as the Army's Headquarters in Scotland were located at the end of the runway. I was then working on the Army press desk and the Army was very relaxed about the matter. Its offices were double-glazed and, in any case, staff had worked in much noisier places around the world.

The Scotsman's reporter rang me to ask for the Army's comment on this runway extension. I said the Army was not concerned. There were many places in the world where airplanes, runways and people lived in much closer proximity than was to be found in Edinburgh. I quoted the cases of Hong Kong where planes virtually slalomed through the skyscrapers to land and take off, and Luqa in Malta where planes took off right over the local parish church. Also improvements in building noise insulation meant the perceived noise nuisance was virtually non-existent. At the end of a long and amiable chat, the reporter thanked me.

The next day, the Army HQ sent me a copy of the cutting (no faxes in those days). The report was all about how relaxed the Army was about the runway extension, with ample quotations to support the Army view. The groups who had initiated the story and expected their views to be the main, if not the whole, part of the story found that I had hijacked it and that they were relegated to a two-sentence balance quotation at the end of the news report. The Army HQ in Scotland was delighted that an awkward incident had been averted and I had a friend on *The Scotsman* who for years afterwards was only too pleased to take news stories from me.

News appeal - the human angle

People like reading about people. Have you noticed how newspapers always include people's home towns, their ages and interests? The apocryphal headline seen in a student charity magazine captures the essence of a perfect headline, 'Sex change Vicar, 46, in Home Counties Woodland Orgy'. Who could resist the temptation to buy a newspaper with that headline?

The first lesson in effective use of media relations is to look for the human angle. How many companies have had their sales success, research and development accomplishments, export successes, and key appointment announcements die a death in the news editor's enormous waste paper bin because they forgot the human interest? Did the workforce give up their Bank Holiday weekend to deliver on time? Did the company's tea lady work overtime, even producing home-made cakes, so work could continue non-stop? If any of that occurred, the wise PR manager will highlight the human angle.

Another sensitive human angle is employment. Try to include news which says that business has led to an increase in employment or extra business for sub-contractors, or even that it will lead to an increase in something unexpected such as tourism.

Even in a disaster situation, proper management of the human interest angle can minimise damage. A classic example was when a submarine 'sank' whilst alongside its jetty in Gosport. The Royal Navy PR Officer (PRO), a highly experienced Government Information Officer, dashed off down to the naval base to find guards on the gate barring all visitors from entering the site and the Commanding Officer told him to keep the press out. Despite the Commanding Officer's seniority, the PRO advised him to let the press in under his supervision. In came the press into a rapidly established press office, complete with bacon butties and coffee. Fortunately, no one died. All those on board were rescued by two Petty Officer divers. As the press wanted a story, the PRO decided he would give them one, but the one he wanted them to have. So every 15 or 20 minutes thoughout the night, one of the divers would come in and give the press an update on the rescue. The next day, the newspapers were full of the two hero-divers who had rescued everyone from the sunken submarine. The reason that the submarine had sunk, negligence, was completely overlooked.

Fortunately for business, news editors are now aware of the importance of industry and commerce, not just for the economic well-being of the country or region, but also as a source of good copy. As a result, business news receives its fair share of coverage. Looking at one of the 'heavies' of 30 years ago, there were about three pages of business news, including a page of share prices. Today, the heavies devote two to three times more space to business and even the 'red tops' (tabloids) now have a page or two devoted to it. But never forget, these pages need to be filled for every edition (as do all newspaper pages), and news from business as well as government departments, quangos, charities and other organisations are a prime source of copy. So now comes the major question, how do you make sure your news is used in preference to others? Every day the average national news editor receives about 600 press releases. All of them cost much the same to produce and about 590 of them go straight into the waste paper bin. How to save your press release from being thrown away is the subject of Chapter 9.

Giving your story eye appeal

We all know that a picture is worth a thousand words. We all know that a good sound bite will be given good coverage. But beware, the opposite is equally relevant; the botched up quotation can attract equally comprehensive coverage, but normally with adverse effects for the source.

On a NATO exercise in Denmark, I was in the exercise press office looking for a human interest story. I was finding this difficult as it was just another NATO exercise, yawn! yawn! Yes, it was of vital importance to all the participants, but was it to the outside world? As a result, we asked all the units for human-interest stories and we were overwhelmed by a deafening silence, except from a TA Gunner regiment in Wales. A Bombardier had proposed to his Gunner girlfriend on board the ferry to Denmark. Perhaps, said one of the officers, it might make a story. In minutes, we were in a Land Rover burning rubber across Zealand. On the way there we went through the village of Løve (Danish for lion). At the regimental HQ we tried to take a number of photos of the couple that encapsulated the event and the context of a major NATO exercise involving 10,000 soldiers. None of them really worked, so we bundled them into the back of the Land Rover and drove to Løve where we stood them behind the village sign, his arm around her. The story was used in no fewer than 26 UK newspapers and even one Danish newspaper carried it. Of course, it made the news because of the photograph, but they all carried the key message that these two TA soldiers were on a NATO exercise with 10,000 troops.

He proposed to her on a ferry to Denmark while on a multi-national NATO exercise. Fortunately, the village of Løve was nearby for the souvenir picture and the resulting story was published in 26 newspapers, including a Danish daily newspaper that appreciated the play on the word, despite the fact that Løve means lion.

Press briefing conventions

When one talks to the press there are some conventions and jargon, which once assimilated, will make the task much more relaxed. The first rule is that a journalist can only report what he sees or hears. He does not express opinions (his sources might); the newspaper's editorial does that. In doing so, the reporter is reporting 'attributable' news, i.e. he has an identifiable source of news and facts. Sometimes the term 'on the record' is used. So the first rule when talking to journalists is to assume that everything you say can be used 'on the record' and published, perhaps even against your interests.

If you are very experienced and, better still, know the journalist, you can use some other conventions. When you use them, state them right at the beginning, not in the middle or the end of a briefing or interview; by then it is too late.

'Off the record' or 'for background use' mean that the information is literally for background and guidance, not for publication. It is often used by the interviewee or briefer to set the background against which the interview or facts are set. It enables the journalist to reflect the feel of the story, perhaps the interviewee's frustration, delight, etc.

'Unattributable' means that the comment cannot be attributed to an identified source, rather it can be used with only a hint of the actual source. Typically a news report might refer to 'government' or 'industry' sources predicting a course of action or making a comment. Watch out for news reports in the lead-up to a government reshuffle, or trailing budget proposals, when government sources indicate that a minister is likely to face a move, up, down or sideways, or that tax bands might change. In the course of a lobbying campaign, pressure groups might give unattributable quotations, such as 'industry sources indicated a lack of confidence in the poorly thought-out proposals'. For most businessmen there will be precious few opportunities to use unattributable comment to full effect, but if you do, make sure your PR adviser is alongside you to ensure that you have prefaced your comment as unattributable, and that the reporter is fully aware of that.

'Embargoes' are applied to news reports ahead of the time of publication. They are to be used for the convenience of the press and not for the convenience of the company or organisation releasing the news. By giving a weighty report to the press early in the morning, embargoed not for use until the afternoon, this gives the press time to digest it and give it more detailed coverage, which is appreciated by the journalists concerned. Sometimes it is advisable to tell the press, for operational planning purposes only, that such a report is due a few days earlier so that the news editor can start to plan his diary for the day well in advance. Sometimes the wise PR adviser will arrange some embargoed press facilities in the days ahead of the event so they will have photos and even TV footage in the can, edited ready for transmission, immediately after the embargo time.

Embargoed press releases should quite clearly state on the head of the press release the following: 'Embargo. Not for use until (time and date)'. Embargoes are respected as a matter of course. Those that are broken tend to be the ones where there has been an overly long embargo time.

In PR, one is often confronted with the turgid, boring, routine stuff to publicise. But no matter how dull the story, use your initiative and imagination; think like a reporter. How would you attract the reader's attention? It is not impossible; be prepared to be hard nosed or else all your effort will end up with the other 590 failed press releases in the news editor's waste paper bin.

Chapter 3
The print media

The written word traces its roots back to the Sumerian cuneiform script, when society had become sufficiently complex to necessitate some form of recording events, regulations, laws, etc. Perhaps the earliest known forms of using writing to influence other people with the aim of gaining a pre-determined reaction is the graffiti found on the walls within the ruins of Pompeii where various aspiring politicians wrote their appeals to the voters on the walls. As writing rather limited the number of books that could be produced and the vast majority of the population was illiterate, the use of the written word to influence large numbers of people had to wait until the 15th century when Caxton invented moveable type for printing. The earliest printed products that carried contemporary news were broadsheets reporting something of immediate interest, such as the latest batch of unfortunates on their way to Tyburn. From these broadsheets developed newspapers and magazines that we know today, although it was not until the newspaper tax was repealed in the latter half of the 19th century that newspapers became really cheap and readily available to everyone. Over time, newspapers have evolved to appeal to their different readerships. A basic knowledge of the print media will help in understanding how best to use them.

Local weekly newspapers

The last 30 years have seen the emergence of hundreds of free weekly newspapers, which in many cases are normally an excellent medium for advertising (and rely on it for survival). However, the more influential amongst the weekly newspapers are the paid-for weeklies. There are hundreds of them in the UK, covering all the parish pump tittle-tattle, which is what the readers actually want to read. Within many of these newspapers' circulation areas are normally a great number of businesses, all the source of much interesting local news. Unfortunately, businessmen do not seem to think it worthwhile to develop relationships with local journalists and to raise the profile of their own companies within their locality. What these businessmen tend to forget is that one of their most important audiences, their employees, tend to be absolutely delighted when their company is in the local paper. It is a great morale booster.

Many journalists start their careers on local newspapers and when they move on to other newspapers their views on many aspects of life will have been influenced by their first experiences. The positive way you deal with the local press can pay dividends much later on when the local journalist is on a national newspaper and takes business news seriously, as a source of not only good copy but also for good readership response.

It is vital for local businessmen to remember exactly what the local press want. They want a local angle as the readership want local news. The more local angles you can incorporate into the story, the better. When I was a commercial graduate trainee with Thomson Regional Newspapers, one of the memorable incidents was watching the night distribution manager in action. He would look at every story in every page and assess just how many extra copies it might sell. He would look at a wedding photograph, preferably with all the guests. There might be 18 faces in the photograph, all of them wanting souvenir copies of the paper, so he would 'box out' about 36 extra copies to the newsagents in the area, knowing that most would be taken and the majority of newsagents expected box outs, as it meant extra business for them. Nearly every story would be looked at and extra copies boxed out accordingly. This particular newspaper had a circulation of about 100,000 and every night about 600 extra copies would be boxed out. Eventually all these box outs would help the newspaper increase its circulation, at which point it could then charge more for advertising. So the canny businessman should incorporate as many local links as possible so that the story is not just newsworthy in its own right, but it also gives the newspapers the opportunity to sell more copies.

Many local newspapers are run on a shoestring with virtually minimal journalistic staff. They do not have time to edit excessively wordy press releases; these are the ones that are spiked or binned immediately. Press releases that have been written ready to be dropped straight into the paper have nearly every chance of being used.

As has already been mentioned, many local reporters offer their stories to the national press. If you look in any national newspaper you will see that almost two-thirds of all stories are from local news reporters across the country. So there are opportunities that your story could well make it into a national newspaper.

Regional newspapers

These newspapers are very influential. They tend to have the monopoly in the area as the morning, evening or Sunday newspaper. They have healthy circulations and a good readership. There are about 90 of these newspapers covering the whole country. Nearly all of them have specialist financial and business reporters and many of them are based in London. No matter where you are or what you are, a single- or a multi-site company, you can offer your news to local newspapers with local angles to appeal to each of them.

When you decide which newspaper to approach, morning, evening or Sunday, bear in mind that each has its district readerships. The morning papers have a wide geographical distribution and the readership tends to be more business-orientated than the evening papers. As the first editions go to bed at about 7.30 pm the night before, a distribution manager has more time to send the newspapers to fairly far-flung areas. Having arrived there, the morning papers have a fairly long shelf-life, from about 6.00 am to about 2.00 pm, when the evening papers then arrive.

The evening papers, by comparison, circulate within a much tighter area, typically a city and its immediate suburbs. Production starts at about 9.00 am with the first edition hitting the streets at about midday, the second edition mid-afternoon and the final edition at about 4.45 pm. Each edition has a short shelf-life and in some cases, the final edition may only have a shelf-life of 30 minutes, as it is designed for the worker at the end of the day leaving the office, picking up his evening paper, packet of cigarettes, etc. So beware of distribution managers who fail to deliver the evening paper by 4.45 pm, as the newsagent not only loses the paper sale but also the other items bought at the same time. However, the good news for businessmen is that evening newspapers reach a very high proportion of the population within the circulation area, sometimes as high as 85 per cent, which means there is a greater cross-section of the population likely to see the paper.

Then there are the local Sunday newspapers. Again their main selling point is local appeal, but like all Sunday papers, the news is well leavened with entertaining reading, ranging from gardening to travel. For local businessmen, there are a few points to remember when dealing with all Sunday papers. Firstly, Monday is their day off, and their reporters do not attend press conferences and press facilities. Secondly, the paper is virtually complete with features, etc by Friday lunchtime, leaving Saturday free for the collection of news for the hard news columns.

So ultimately any businessman wanting his fair share of news coverage should make contact with the business reporters from his local papers, and cultivate at least one of them. Every time you make contact, be it a visit to the factory or a meeting in a pub, do not waste his time. The reporter wants news, he has to fill the newspaper, so make sure that at every meeting you have some interesting hard news. The journalist will then know that you are a source of news and will respond all the more readily to you.

The leading regional newspapers have an understated influence, sometimes well beyond their circulation areas - not only do they cover local business, but also national business and industrial organisations. These influential newspapers include *The Scotsman*, *The Belfast Telegraph*, *The Western Mail*, *Birmingham Post* and *The Press and Journal*. In many cases, these papers have a London office and the reporters there are normally only too pleased when contacts are cultivated giving them a London story with a local peg on which to hang it.

The nationals

These are the well-known dailies and the Sundays. They are split into the 'heavies' and the 'red tops'. The heavies specialise in quality, in-depth reporting, and they invariably are overwhelmed with news from a huge variety of sources. A typical news editor on a national newspaper receives about 600 press releases a day, of which three or four might be used. The volume of incoming news is just as vast for the business editors on the City desks. Fortunately, the effect of this increased flow of news aimed at City desks has resulted in the nationals devoting more space to business news as they know there is a readership that will buy newspapers for comprehensive business news coverage.

Whilst the nationals cover national and international news in some depth, close inspection of the by-lines will show that about one-third of the news will have been credited to its own reporters and the remainder to local newspapers and news agencies (Reuters, Press Association, Associated Press, etc). With such a choice of news, editors can be very choosy about what they cover.

The City pages of the heavies and the red tops have, naturally, a different style of reporting business news. The red tops will be short, snappy and will reflect their own style of reporting. However, do not decry the difference in style. Red top business pages are a major source of business news for millions of small shareholders.

The good news is that many reporters on the nationals are just as approachable as their opposite numbers on the regionals. So keeping in contact through good and bad times means that when bad news breaks, they will listen to you and give you an opportunity to soften the blow.

The Sunday newspapers

The modus operandi of the Sundays is much the same as their national counterparts and their deadlines are much the same as the regional Sundays. Unlike their daily counterparts, their news coverage is of smaller proportion, but they have all week, if not longer, to research and write much deeper reports and features.

The good news is that nearly all of them comprise a fistful of supplements, with at least one of them dedicated solely to business. Very recently, *The Sunday Business* was established to cater specifically for the business market and it has a healthy circulation.

'It's no exaggeration to say that your press release has flown to the very top of my in-tray'.

Technical and trade press

Pick up any reference book, such as Benns or Pims, on the media and be prepared to be amazed by the number of specialist magazines it lists. There are thousands of them: bee keeping, anti-corrosion, technical textiles, haematology, defence electronics and even public finance initiatives, all with their avid readership and all of them having to fill the pages for each edition to hold the readers' interest. Some have sizeable readerships and should not be excluded. Maintain contact with these and the businessman will find that the ability to transmit detailed information to target specialist audiences is much eased.

Writing for the specialist press is different from writing for the mainstream news media. Whereas the news media want the news in a set form for ease of editing (see Chapter 2), the specialist magazine prefers to receive material written in a feature format, preferably in its house style, complete with graphics, photographs and illustrations.

In the City, many analysts in the broking houses and investment banks read the specialist press for the detail on how a company is developing its business. When I worked for a major defence electronics company, *Electronics Weekly* and *Electronics Times* were invited to all press briefings, conferences and facilities. They gave the company extensive coverage of all aspects of the business, but the company knew that it had an extra line of communication with the City analysts who we knew were always fully informed. Having these two key magazines on our side meant we had two valuable allies in the media. So when we were subject to a hostile takeover bid, these two magazines were fully supportive of our resistance. Despite the fact that after 11 months we were taken over, one of the magazines continued to be critical of the takeover for two or three years afterwards.

Consumer press

The range of the consumer press reflects the range of activities of the British public. Included in this are magazines on weddings, car restoration, celebrities, cycling, etc, as well as all the women's and men's magazines. Whilst these might appear to be of limited use to the business trying to explain its success, they should always be considered, as they can be invaluable in supporting the marketing of a company's products.

Chapter 4
Television

What you'll find in this chapter:

➡ Programme checklist
➡ Codes of conduct
➡ Interviews
➡ Presentation

The numbers of people TV, radio and increasingly the Internet (the 'electronic media') can reach are immense; collective reaction to them shape mass perception. These three types of media will be discussed in the next few chapters, but first, let's begin with the huge influence of television.

Who can forget the visual impact of Michael Burke's moving and sensitive news report on the BBC of the famine in Sudan, with pictures of young children picking flakes of dried food from the outside of the cooking pots? It resulted in an incredible outpouring of public sympathy and the relief agencies were swamped with donations. As you know, TV and radio can be powerful means of communication, but the time the average businessman has to put across his message can be as little as 30 or 40 seconds.

Not only may the businessman have only a limited amount of time, but there is such a proliferation of channels, he has to make sure he is not only on the right channel for the right audience but also at the right time. With terrestrial, satellite, cable and Internet TV channels all competing for our attention, all with their specialist programmes, plus the enormous selection of radio stations, businessmen and even their PR advisers may have a problem in identifying the best channels.

Some years ago, a group of PR specialists was discussing the best use of PR. One recounted how pleased his client was to have had his annual awards ceremony the subject of a 30-minute programme on a regional TV station at 11.00 pm. A colleague said it might well have been excellent for the client, well at least the client's ego, but he had been involved in publicising a tobacco-sponsored nautical awards ceremony that resulted in a total of some 20 minutes on local TV stations' evening programmes, along with well over an hour of radio coverage and several hundred press clippings. The late-night programme was a one-off and, compared with the early-evening programmes, it had a minuscule audience. The tobacco-sponsored award ceremony, on the other hand, was also an annual event, but a three-month run up programme of news releases had been produced, which raised press interest most effectively, so that the TV and radio coverage were all at prime time when the audiences were at their maximum and the print press coverage was equally high profile. Both events had much the same budget, but the more successful one followed the basic tenet of PR - 'a planned and sustained programme'.

However, there are times when satellite, cable and Internet TV can be of use. A tobacco client was sponsoring the Jaguar team at Le Mans and he desperately wanted to be on TV. He gave us a healthy budget to achieve the aim. As part of my research, I went to a satellite TV show at Wembley. The two-acre car park was absolutely wall-to-wall with satellite dishes. Inside the exhibition hall were hundreds of TVs showing thousands of satellite TV programmes from around the world. Three weeks later, we met our client and returned 60 per cent of his budget, saying we had arranged for him to be on two TV stations. The great advantage was that both stations planned to show the Le Mans live, with lengthy highlights repeated eight times. Most satellite and cable channels may well have a large number of subscribers, but they do not all view the race at the same time. So by repeating the highlights we were sure that a worthwhile number of people would see the event. Perhaps the best part was the postscript: one of the cars broke down and our client was distraught. Then we showed him the relevant footage. There was the broken down Silk Cut Jaguar limping slowly back to the pits with the cameras following it all the way for three or four minutes, with all the branding and sponsorship logos very clearly visible, compared to the blurs of the other cars as they whizzed past the cameras at more than 180 mph. So the client had more than 70 minutes of transmission time where his sponsored car could be clearly seen by the audiences in two of his key marketing areas.

TV audiences are not only very large, but their ability to absorb information ranges from the totally focused to the wholly disinterested, and will include many who have difficulty in understanding the simplest programmes, let alone more complex ones that involve news and business. So the businessman with his 30 or 40 seconds has to think very carefully about what he wants to say, preferably using the lowest common denominator so he is understood by the maximum number of people.

Even if he succeeds in attracting the audience's interest, he still has to remember to maintain a sustained programme of communication, otherwise the audience will forget. This problem is not just peculiar to businesses and similar organisations. Government departments have the same problems. When I was in the Government Information Service, I was in discussion with the Information Officer in the British Consulate in San Francisco. The task was to put the British Government's policy on Northern Ireland across in California, in order to undermine support for the IRA. The Information Officer summed up the problem succinctly, saying there were so many news channels on TV and radio that if we were lucky there might be 20 minutes a month covering the whole of Northern Ireland out of the total of 43,200 minutes. How much of that would be remembered? He hazarded a guess at not very much at all. What would be remembered would be the bombing and other highly televisual atrocities which the stations were looking to screen to capture the viewers.

Programme checklist

Having sounded almost disparaging about the problems of appearing on TV, businessmen can swing the effect of appearing on TV to their advantage by remembering three things:

- Firstly, is it prime time?

- Secondly, if it is not, is it the specialist programme that your target audiences will be watching?

- Thirdly, make sure that you have quite clearly decided what you are going to say. Steer clear of discussion programmes; daytime TV is seldom watched by the movers and shakers, and take care over accepting invitations to some satellite and cable TV programmes as their audiences may be so small, it may not be worth the effort to appear on them.

Appearing on prime TV could well mean that you will be seen by millions of people. Remember the old adage that a picture can tell a thousand words, so beware of the following:

- The snazzy tie you received at Christmas can detract attention away from you.

- If you wear spectacles, make sure they are pushed well up your nose so the top of the frame does not obscure your eyes.

- Do not wear tinted glasses or even the most fashionable of shades; either way you will look shifty or untrustworthy.

A cockpit simulator to replicate the movements of flying, at Cranfield Aerospace. The poster in the background helps to establish the location.

- By all means make sure you have some establishing background like your bottling plant or the company sign by the factory entrance.

- Wear distracting clothing or display eye-catching mannerisms and the viewers' attention to your carefully chosen words will be lost.

- Whilst many of us may like a drink on social occasions or with a meal, do not drink when you are likely to appear on TV. Alcohol opens up the veins in your epidermis and allows more blood into the vessels below your skin. You then look pinkish or blushing red and it will be picked up by the camera. Anyone appearing in a TV programme or an interview needs to be able to respond as quickly as possible to events, lucidly and briefly.

Codes of conduct

Both the BBC and the independent TV companies have codes of conduct that give you certain rights, once you agree to appear on TV. Is it a live programme or recorded? Is it a discussion programme with a friendly or hostile audience? Ask the producer or interviewer about the likely line of questioning; it helps you to prepare your answers and keeps hesitancy to a minimum, especially if you are facing complex questions.

Before you go into the studio or appear in front of the camera, go to the toilet. Here you can have a few moments privacy to think through the questions and answers, check your hair, adjust your tie or blouse and perhaps wash your face to remove any unsightly grime or sweat. You may be made up by the studio make-up artist, and they prefer to apply make-up onto clean skin.

The interviews

At work

There are four types of interviews businessmen, and indeed many others, are inclined to be invited to do. The most likely is the interview at work. For TV companies, this provides the opportunity to catch some of your business activity on film or video to provide a suitable backdrop for the introductory voiceover before the interview itself. So be prepared to show the TV crew and interviewer around, preferably to those areas that show the company in its most positive light and are naturally interesting. Such interviews, with a supporting introduction and interview, will be about two to four minutes long in a 30 minute local news magazine programme, usually transmitted at lunchtime or in the early evening.

Try to decide just where you want the interview to take place. Look at a few local TV interviews from the factory, business or office. In many cases, the interviewee is positioned by the main company sign or has the factory or even delivery van in the immediate background. This helps to establish the interview location, otherwise the interviewee might just as well be a talking head.

With these interviews, as always, discuss the line of questioning with the interviewer so you are mentally ready with your answers and be prepared for the final unexpected question at the end. Make sure the location of the interview is not in a noisy area. If it is taking place in your office, take the phone off the hook and have someone outside the door to stop people barging in. Also, be prepared for the TV crew possibly moving your office furniture around, although invariably they will replace it. When TV interviews are conducted in your office or place of work, they are almost always recorded. If it is and you make a complete mess of an answer, do not hesitate to say that you would like to do it again. The interviewer will almost always agree, as he will want a good interview and will not want to show you as incompetent.

When TV crews ask to interview you, invite them to come at a time most convenient to them. You are likely to receive some positive exposure, so readjust your diary to make it easy for the TV crew. Remember, they will have several stories to cover in a day and, like a good salesman's territory, they will try to plan their day to fit in as many calls as possible with minimum travelling time between them.

In the studio

The TV studio is a well-lit space with a backdrop, somewhere for the interviewer and interviewee to sit, two or three cameras gliding around the floor, two or three people with radio headsets and clipboards, the floor manager and assistants and in the background, in a glass box to one side, is the programme producer. On arrival at the studio, you should meet the producer who will explain the aim of the programme and will introduce you to the interviewer. Use the time with the producer and the interviewer to ask questions about any areas of the programme which you are uncertain about and the line of questioning they intend to take with you.

When you go into the studio for the interview, do not smoke. The fire regulations forbid it, and besides, it does not create a good impression to the viewers.

When you sit down in the studio, make sure you are in a static chair; a swivel chair provides all sorts of distracting movements - distracting for the audience and distracting for you. Do not touch anything as all of it will have been carefully set up. You will then be asked to say something in order to check the sound level, so say something innocuous such as what you had for breakfast.

Once you have a couple of interviews under your belt, it is then more likely that you will be invited into the TV studio for interviews. They may be straight news interviews of just a few minutes, but they will be live. Be confident, you know the subject - your business - better than the interviewer, no matter how well he has researched the subject.

Check on all the facts before you arrive at the studio and have the key points you must put across clear in your mind. Give honest answers and when you do not know the answer, admit it, as such honesty is appreciated. Do not waffle and precede your answer with 'I'm glad you asked me that, it is a difficult question, but...' This wastes time and loses you the opportunity to make pertinent points. It also undermines your attractiveness to being invited back for more interviews and anyone in their right mind tries to keep open their lines of communication with TV and radio stations.

Unfortunately, you are most likely to be invited to a studio interview when there are problems within your business. The most probable is an industrial dispute. These are occasions when the management only wants to say what is already public. Do not discuss your negotiations on the airwaves. However, your management team can say a lot without compromising them. If you have to give negative answers in front of the camera be prepared to explain why: 'We are still negotiating. It would be wrong for the company to speculate on the outcome of the negotiations, but we are part of the local community and we want the company and its employees to be successful and enjoy the benefits of success'.

Listen carefully to the questions, answer lucidly and briefly and do not let your tongue run away. Answer the question and perhaps add an extra comment that strengthens your case. You are in the picture at all times; ignore the cameras and concentrate on the interviewer. It is quite easy and after a few seconds you will forget the surrounding paraphernalia of the studio and talk quite naturally to the interviewer.

Do not gesticulate as it is very distracting. As the camera is on your face, use facial expressions to reflect your feelings, smile but do not smirk, nod in agreement but do not scowl, basically look as if you are in control of the interview and the subject matter. Do not tell jokes.

At the end of the interview, always assume you are still on camera until you are out of the studio or the outside camera has been switched off. Numerous people have assumed the interview has finished and have started to tell jokes, commented that they are so pleased not to be asked about something embarrassing or they make disparaging remarks about the interview subject not realising the cameras are still running. When this happens, it is bonus time for the interviewer. The material is fair game for transmission and the carefully crafted interview will be binned and the embarrassing off-the-cuff remarks used instead. Well, fair enough, it will be far more entertaining material for the viewers than a routine interview.

Down the line

As much as TV and radio stations like to interview people in a studio or with their cameras or own tape recorders, there are occasions when that is not possible and you may well be asked to do a down the line interview. Sometimes TV stations have a remote studio where you sit in a small studio with an unmanned camera staring you in the face and an earpiece connecting you to the interviewer. All the points about TV interviews apply equally to a down the line interview, but instead of being fussed around by the producer, the floor manager, etc, you take all your instructions over the earpiece.

Discussion programmes

The opportunities for businessmen to be invited on discussion programmes increase as more and more channels, terrestrial, satellite, cable and Internet try to fill their transmission schedules with programmes. When you receive an invitation to a discussion programme, assess the audience and whether it is worth appearing in front of them. A discussion programme between 9.00 am and 12.30 pm probably does not have the sort of audience that will be interested in your business. However, between 12.30 pm and 2.00 pm, there are a number of business oriented discussion programmes which are worthwhile and again any after 6.00 pm.

These programmes are not an opportunity for debating issues. It provides you with an opportunity to put across your point of view. Stay within the bounds of your knowledge and when asked about matters outside your knowledge limits, admit it politely, perhaps saying that you cannot add any more.

Presentation

Remember the Zeebrugge ferry disaster? There were four main players in that tragedy. The ferry company, the Department of Transport, the Belgian rescue services and the British Army. The Department of Transport swung into action immediately with its duty press officer appearing very rapidly at the office with his sleeping bag, successfully advising Ministers and officials on how to manage the press. The Belgian rescue services were in immediate action and were seen to be doing their job. The Army was involved because one of its units was returning on the ferry from its posting in Germany and the next of kin were, naturally, highly concerned. By chance, the Army was on a huge 'desk exercise' over the weekend on which the disaster happened and it had all the key people in place to manage the personnel and news media aspects of the disaster. Unfortunately, the ferry company was caught flatfooted, and if it had a contingency plan, it was not obvious.

The most memorable aspect of the ferry company's reaction was the appearance on the TV news of the Chief Executive who, I will always remember, was wearing an incredibly large brown velvet trilby-style hat. I cannot remember what he said, but his personal presentation and style of speaking did not engender confidence in his command of the situation. It is to the ferry company's credit that it very soon acknowledged it had no company capability to manage the media in a crisis. So a few months later it headhunted the same Department of

Transport's duty press officer, having seen him in action so successfully in the months of post mortems and enquiries after the disaster.

At the other end of the scale of disaster management was British Midlands air crash at Kegworth. Very promptly, Sir Michael Bishop, the airline's Chief Executive, was at the site of the crash, sensibly attired, available for interview by all and sundry. He knew what he had to say and he said it with confidence and gave every indication that the airline management had the confidence and capability to handle all aspects of the crash and its aftermath. It was a masterly performance which has positively supported the airline's reputation ever since. This is how one should present oneself on television.

Chapter 5
Radio

Perhaps the most famous early incident that showed the immediate impact the electronic media can have on the public was in 1938. An American radio station was broadcasting H G Wells' *War of the Worlds*. The quality of production, done almost in news reporting style, caused consternation across the USA, as listeners tuned in after the start of the programme and believed the earth really was being invaded. There was widespread panic across the country, that died down almost as quickly as it had started once the programme had finished.

Radios can make such an impact because they are ubiquitous. Recent surveys have found that every household has about six radios, plus one in every car. The BBC has five national channels and ITN provides the news for many of the independent radio stations. There are some independent radio stations that have national coverage, but the majority of stations, including BBC, only cover a region. Even in the UK, there are hundreds of radio stations. Many of them just produce aural wallpaper, virtually non-stop music, with on-the-hour news headlines, whilst others are highly specialised be it in music, language, etc. For some communication activity, such as advertising, all radio stations should be considered, especially if they have a good coverage of your target audience. Then there are the international radio stations such as the *BBC World Service*, *Deutch Welle* and *Voice of America*.

Radio news gathering is similar to TV, only that it has a long history of being able to report news instantly. Radio is not limited to newspaper deadlines, where there is a massive logistic in gathering news, producing the copy, printing the paper and distributing the various editions to newsagents and other retail outlets. TV output is programmed for a variety of programmes during the day, some news and some current affairs. Radio, on the other hand, can and does have news on the hour and every hour. In times of crisis, the news will be every half an hour.

Perhaps you might have seen the film *The Battle of the River Plate*. There is the memorable sight of an American radio reporter taking over a riverside bar's telephone and providing a non-stop commentary on events of the sea battle as they unfolded to his radio station in New York. The broadcast was a source of much embarrassment to the Germans and a source of diplomatic pressure for the British. Another more recent example of a radio station's flexibility to deal with the totally unexpected was the death of the Princess of Wales, when several radio stations ran non-stop coverage for most of that Sunday.

For effective corporate communications, businessmen should use the stations that carry worthwhile news programmes with the right target audience. You should listen carefully to the interviews; fairly soon you will start to notice the factors that make a good one, because you are aware that your interest has been gained. A good interviewee speaks in short factual sentences, which makes it easier for the radio journalist to edit if necessary. Answers are refreshingly clear with qualifications as to why such a course of action was taken, unless it happens to support the coffee cup effect. The coffee cup effect? This is the sort of interest grabbing comment that makes you stop sipping your coffee, or your razor stops in mid-air as you listen with fascinated interest.

Handling interviews

Whilst you can appear at a radio studio for an interview in dirty gardening clothes, fully aware that the listeners cannot see you, you should make a habit of turning up looking neat, tidy and smart. It will actually make a favourable impression on the radio reporter who then will be more willing to invite you back for further interviews. However, there are the verbal equivalents of distracting clothing and eye-catching mannerisms. My most memorable distraction was listening to a senior police officer being interviewed on Radio 4's *Today* programme. As I listened I heard him repeat the phrase 'at this moment in time'. So I started to count and I believe he repeated the phrase seven times. The next day in the letters column of the *Daily Telegraph*, a reader wrote in to say he had heard the interview and was astounded to hear the police officer use the phrase 'at this moment in time' nine times in a three-minute interview. I doubt if anyone can remember what the police officer was talking about, but for a large number of people he will always be remembered as Mr. Nine Times 'at this moment in time'.

Radio stations tend to be run on a shoestring; reporters do not have company cars, or lavish expense accounts, or time to leave the studio for routine-type interviews. But they do need news, just like all the other media. So the secret to success with local radio stations is to phone up and offer to come round to the studio and be interviewed. In the vast majority of cases, such offers for interviews about real news will be very welcome. So turn up at the allotted time for the interview. Do not expect the red carpet and the best china with your cup of coffee. You will be expected to find your way to the studio, there will be a curt hello, and a hand will point to the coffee or, if you are really lucky, someone will pour it out into a plastic beaker. Don't be offended; plastic cups do not make a chinking or clunking noise which then intrude into the microphone.

On one occasion, I took a Minister of State to Broadcasting House for an interview. Once in the producer's office, we had a quick brief on the interview, the plastic cup of ubiquitous coffee appeared, and then we, complete with a large, important and amiable Minister, had to wander around the building looking for a spare studio. After a quick three-minute recorded interview, it was out of the building. It seemed almost casual to the point of curtness, but the Minister had an important point to make publicly, the BBC wanted to carry it and that was only three minutes of the day's output. So do not be surprised if you go through a radio studio and are treated like a sausage in a production line.

Be prepared for the unexpected and have a substitute available if your number one choice for interviewee is not available. Whilst working with the company Plessey, I managed to get a report on the company's new portable minehunting system on the *Today* programme's 7.00 am news. This amazing piece of kit was a nine-foot long, yellow submarine at the end of a 1,000-yard long control cable. It swam in front of its ship, which could be anything from a trawler to an enormous oil tanker, and could detect and find mines on the sea bed or tethered in the water. As the Persian Gulf had been heavily mined at that time, the launch of this system had a good peg on which to hang the story, hence the success of having it reported on the news. Minutes later at 7.35 am, the *Today* editor phoned me and asked for the Plessey expert to come in immediately for an interview. Two minutes later I discovered he was away from home, so I phoned the studio. 'Who else is there?' was the reply. 'Well, me actually,' I replied; 20 minutes later I was in the interview studio in Broadcasting House doing a recorded interview whilst the news was being read; 10 minutes later my two-and-a-half minute interview was broadcast, unedited, with the suitable intro and outro. It resulted in American radio and TV stations doing follow-on reports, numerous newspaper calls for information, the BBC 9 O'Clock News (as was) carried a two-minute special feature on the system and about eight oil tanker companies phoned up Plessey wanting to order the system for their ships.

On another occasion, I held a pre-Farnborough Air Show press conference that went very well. At the end, one of the Technical Directors gave an interview to a radio reporter. Afterwards, the Technical Director commented that the reporter asked some incredibly simple but incisive questions over about five minutes, and wondered on the value of that interview. I was delighted to inform him that the interviewer was the Defence Correspondent of the BBC World Service and within a few hours' time his interview would be broadcast to an audience of 140 million worldwide. The Technical Director just shook his head in amazement.

The Eurofighter was launched at the Farnborough Air Show, and British Aerospace Systems invited the then Secretary of State for Defence, George Robertson to see the plane and meet the test pilots. A well angled photograph captures the establishing background of the tail plane and clear views of the faces.

Just because you can be live on the radio from your telephone, don't forget to handle requests for radio interviews just like a TV or newspaper interview. Go through a simple checklist:

- The subject of the interview.

- The programme in which it will be used.

- The time of transmission.

- Who else is in the programme?

- How long will the interview be?

Even if you are doorstepped at the factory gate or by the entrance to your home, still ask the above questions. If you know those basic facts, you will be in a better position to respond to the request and possibly turn it to your advantage.

Much of what is relevant to TV interviews is relevant to radio interviews, except you must concentrate on the listener. The listener will not know much about your subject or company and your style of delivery should be an almost conversational explanation, but do ensure the key points you want to put across are conveyed.

Damage limitation

Interviews on TV and radio can be highly efficient in projecting a company or an individual very quickly to a large audience. So far this has just covered those interviews where the news value has been the businessman himself or his company and he has generally been in control of events. There will be times when disaster strikes - an accident, contaminated food, environmental pollution - sometimes potentially criminal or illegal. When that happens, the press will chase you for interviews, footage and photographs. This really comes under the heading of managing the media in a crisis, but the few golden rules about interviews under pressure are equally applicable here.

When you find yourself with radio and TV stations pressing for interviews, you will have to assess the value of making yourself available, taking advice as necessary. Ask yourself: What can I say? What do I want to say? Do I need to say it? If you decide to give an interview under such conditions, remember the reporter will be wanting to dig deeply into the story, probably to a depth to which you do not want to go. If you do decide to grant an interview, then do the following:

- Check whether the interview is to be recorded or live.

- Ask for a written request for the interview with an outline of the intended questions.

- List your answers, including the reasons for being economical with information, e.g. sub judice, commercially confidential, contravention of Stock Exchange rules, awaiting further information, breach of security, etc.

- List the three or four points you know you must make, no matter what the questions.

- Have a pre-interview chat with the reporter to check on the line of questioning so you can be mentally prepared with the answers and minimise the 'umms' and 'errs'.

- Make sure your PR adviser is in your line of sight, so you can see any visual signals to ensure you stay on the straight and narrow.

- Be alert during the interview and make your key points.

- Do not lose your temper.

- Be alert for the final unexpected question that you may be able to answer or that you may wish to parry with a comment such as 'I am waiting for more information', or 'I really need notice of that question so I can answer it for you'.

You all probably will have seen recordings of various businessmen and, in one case, a Cabinet Minister all losing their temper with interviewers. The Cabinet Minister said he was having no more of the interview, unwired himself and walked out. In the other example, a Chief Executive of a utility company said he was having no more of the interview, said he was finished with the questioning and lost his temper. Although instead of walking out, he continued to answer questions and, much to the delight of the interviewer, dug himself further into a hole and did his reputation no good at all.

Radio and TV are amazingly effective at giving a memorable and effective way of transmitting news. It may seem easy, but it can all too often become a disaster because the subject loses the co-ordination between jaw and brain, looks a total mess or lacks the ability to know when to stop.

No matter how well or confident you reckon you are at handling a radio or TV interview, you must scribble down an aide memoire of the points to make. Check some of the points with your head office and never be afraid to take advice from your PR adviser. Even the most experienced Cabinet Ministers take their press secretaries with them to all interviews. After all, if the interview attracts further press interest, the press secretary/PR adviser will be able to take the questions knowing exactly what was in the interview and in what context.

A classic example of doing an interview without advice or ignoring it happened to me several years ago. I was in the Ministry of Defence Press Office thinking of nipping downstairs to the staff canteen for a sandwich when I was phoned by the Hydrographer to the Navy. They had found in Northern Canada the perfectly preserved deep-frozen body of a Royal Navy sailor who had perished on a Polar expedition and they had discovered that his next of kin had not been presented with his Polar Medal. They had since found his great-great-grandnephew and were planning to present it to him in 50 minutes' time. Could I arrange some TV coverage? 30 minutes later I had BBC TV, ITN and a London TV station hotfooting it to the Ministry of Defence. I then dashed to the room where the presentation ceremony was to take place and tried to brief this sailor's great-great-grandnephew on what to say. He would not listen, he was adamant he knew how to handle interviews. He was filmed and the presentation was duly transmitted on all the stations and the only word they managed to carry was 'Fantastic!' The ITN reporter said later that the poor chap just gabbled away inconsequentially and that was the only word that could be used. So do take advice, decide on the points to make, because it will ensure that your jawbone is connected to your brain.

Organising TV and radio technical facilities for pre-arranged interviews or visits

1. Confirm the time or place.

2. Establish contact names (yours and theirs!), addresses and 24-hour telephones.

3. Know the dimensions of the room, acoustics, and power sources.

4. Prepare for numbers:

    *   TV News (usually three - two crew plus reporter)

    *   TV Features (possibly as many as seven or eight)

    *   Radio teams (one or as many as three)

5. Warn security.

6. Get their passes ready and meet them at reception.

7. Arrange car parking.

8.   Offer coffee or light lunch if necessary.

9.   Have the interviewee's brief biography available, and distribute notes with the name, correct title and brief description of their role and function within the company.

10.   Give them as much information as possible.

11.   Think about backgrounds (can the company name be inserted?)

12.   Think about an alternative background too!

13.   Does the team require access to the plant? If so, is specialist transport required for movement inside the factory?

14.   Does the team require a knowledgeable escort on site?

15.   Does the team require a plant electrician in attendance? (Do you have a union problem?)

16.   Do they need special site clothing? (Goggles? Rubber boots? Hard hats? 'Superclean' kit?)

17.   Inform the team of any banned areas and tell them WHY they can't film or record there - but be discreet. Don't inflame curiosity!

18.   Introduce the team to your interviewee/s. (See also *Preparing the company spokesperson* on page 107).

19.   Keep everything as relaxed as possible.

Chapter 6
The Internet

What you'll find in this chapter:

➠ News outlets
➠ Making the most of your site

News outlets

The Internet is the prime source of information for huge numbers of people. There is an increasing number of news outlets who use the World Wide Web as their medium and are just as specialised as their print opposites. Organisations such as *Citywire*, *Bloombergs*, *ADVFN* and even the *FT* provide instant news over the Internet. The numbers who visit these sites or are subscribers can often be considerable, and businessmen and others in PR and corporate communications should include these organisations in their target media outlets. Within the UK, the main Internet news services, such as those mentioned above, specialise in stock market news. This ability to report almost instantly and provide an archive service is invaluable to those working around the stock market, be they fund managers or small, private investors.

With so many new news sites appearing on the Internet, specialised agencies are now in the business of providing a service to companies that want to have their Internet news coverage monitored. This is similar to the services offered by the press cutting agencies, but with the scale and scope of the World Wide Web, it is much more effective to use such a specialised service. The immediacy of news coverage on the Internet can create an immediate reaction to an announcement, and then the next day the coverage in the print media can give a second boost.

With such diversity of media and the ability to search for information, businessmen must take considerable care not to put into the public domain any information that may well be of use to competitor companies. So do not let your enthusiasm for news coverage lead you to leak commercially confidential information to the big wide world, possibly to your detriment.

Making the most of your site

The Internet, that all-pervasive medium that nearly everyone with a computer at home, work or in education uses for correspondence, news gathering, research, advertising or entertainment, is just another communication medium. It is similar to all the other media and should be treated as such. Your press releases can be seen on your company site; your email communications can wing their way around the world, courtesy of cyberspace, for the cost of a local call. Your website can be seen by millions. But how do you attract them to your site and encourage them to respond?

Firstly, and most simply, ensure that all your business communication paper carries your website address and your relevant email addresses. This includes your letterhead, notepaper, business cards, promotional literature, annual report and accounts, etc. In fact, anything you print must include these vital Internet details.

Secondly, make sure that your website is search engine friendly. You can do this in various ways: by publishing in HTML, using key words at the top of the page and repeating key words in the body text, submitting your site details to the main search engines and resubmitting them frequently.

Thirdly, try to be on as many portals as possible without breaking the bank. A portal is an entry point of common interest to relevant websites. A classic portal is CAROL (Company Annual Reports on Line). From www.carol.co.uk one can, within a few seconds, access the online versions of the FTSE 350 company annual reports and accounts on the companies' websites. Once you are there, you can then go deeper into that company's website for further information. I helped to do the publicity for the launch of CAROL in spring 1997. The aim of the campaign was not just to attract companies to use the portal, after all it is free, but to encourage the financial community, brokers, analysts, fund managers, etc, to use the portal as quick and easy access to these annual reports without having to dig them out of the company library. The publicity was extremely successful in attracting users of the portal to access company reports and now the portal carries advert buttons which take users to other sites.

Then there is a range of other factors in using the Internet. Websites should be designed so they can be downloaded quickly and do not assume that emails are a secure means of communication. Internet TV is also increasingly being used but there is room for improvement in the quality of the images.

In addition to the Internet, many companies and organisations have their own Internet, known as an intranet. This provides facilities for a range of internal communications.

In summary, treat the Internet as another medium and apply the normal procedures and practices when incorporating it into your corporate communications programme.

'Pay no attention dear, he's just trying to get us to buy him a new computer again.'

Chapter 7
News agencies

What you'll find in this chapter:

⇒ The Press Association
⇒ Reuters
⇒ Local news agencies
⇒ Internet news agencies

In addition to a news media's own office staff, they will have their own 'stringers', who are freelance reporters paid when they are asked to cover a story or event, and news agencies. News agencies are scattered throughout the world. The best known one in the UK is the Press Association (PA). It has reporters throughout the UK and they report very accurately and objectively on events in their area and file the copy into the PA newsroom in Vauxhall Bridge Road, London. From there it is emailed out to all PA subscribers (nearly all UK newspapers, TV stations, radio stations and a large number of companies). The copy can then be used in the newspapers that consider the news to be pertinent to them. Established in 1868, it is now part of Reuters and is part of a major worldwide news gathering organisation. It has reporters in the press galleries of both the Houses of Parliament; it covers the law courts, sports events and city and financial news.

With its network of some 1,000 correspondents across the UK, PA is able to gather news and, depending on its news value, will put it out on the 'wires' (email subscription service) the same day. The great advantage for business is that PA reporters can cover local business news and it can be transmitted simultaneously to news editors across the country. Make sure you know your local PA reporter and ensure he is on your distribution list for all your news.

The next important new agency is Reuters (which owns PA), the worldwide news agency. It is also the largest in the world and has rapidly widened its services to cover City, financial and business news, as well as running its own business TV channel. If you are launching a news worldwide venture or product with global appeal, then your local Reuters business reporter should be informed and invited to the launch.

Another agency is AP-Dow Jones News Services, a joint venture between the two American agencies, The Associated Press and Dow Jones.

For the local businessman, there are also a number of local news agencies, scouring their area for news and supplying it to regional and national newspapers. There are about 200 local news agencies such as M&Y News agency in Portsmouth, Southern News Service in Surrey and Chester News Service in Chester. These tend to be very good, as they survive on selling news stories to the mainstream newspapers and magazines. Some specialise in business news, others in sport, others in general news, etc. Again keep in touch with those in your area as it will give you a channel to local and national press, as the news desks of the media will have some relationship with them and be prepared to take their copy in preference to press releases.

Freelance journalists, who act like a one-man news agency, do have contacts who are prepared to take their copy. Again keep in touch and ensure they are also on your distribution list. Some of them will cover for specialist trade and technical magazines. They need news, it's their livelihood, so supply it. Often the editor of the local newspaper will also act as a freelance for national newspapers. A classic example of this was about 30 years ago, when the Middlesbrough evening newspaper sent a journalist to cover the world snooker championship held in Teesside. In addition to reporting it for his own paper, he sent his copy to all the national newspapers, who all carried it and the happy journalist earned a good sum for that night's work.

Oracle, Prestel and other TV text news services are now well known. It is well worthwhile, and needs very little effort, to include them in your press release distribution list.

Newcomers to the scene are the Internet news agencies, especially those specialising in business news. These include Citywire, ADVFN, AFX, Bloombergs, Ample Institutional Investor, Hemscott, etc who can take hot news from the Stock Exchange, add some comment and put it out on their websites within minutes; subscribers to their service can have it flashed on their screens immediately. Some of these, such as Bloombergs, publish their own specialist financial magazines in addition to an Internet news service and business television.

You could almost drown in information overload and worry incessantly if you really need to be in contact with all these outlets. But do remember the definition of PR: 'Public relations is the planned, sustained communications between an organisation and its target audiences'.

You should have a good idea which media your target audience reads, watches or listens, so tailor your media list accordingly.

What every news photographer strives to achieve: an action shot with a good establishing background. Shooting against the sun gives dramatic silhouettes. The same action shots can be achieved in an industrial or commercial background with a little imagination.

Chapter 8
Creating a PR strategy

What you'll find in this chapter:

➧ Identifying and researching your target audience
➧ Deciding on your communications strategy
➧ Producing an action plan
➧ Using PR as a marketing tool

If you remember the Institute of Public Relations' definition quoted in the Introduction, then virtually everything required for successful PR will fall into place. At its very simplest, you must identify your target audiences, decide what you want to tell them and how you will inform them. Then you must decide how to maintain the momentum and the information flow. The key points for planning a PR/corporate communications strategy are:

- Identity your target audiences.

- Research their current perceptions of your company product/service.

- Decide on the aim of your communications strategy.

- Decide the key messages you need to put over to your various audiences.

- Identify the means of transmission.

- Decide on the timings to use the various channels to maximum effect.

- Establish what resources are available and required, including people, equipment and money, for publications, advertising, exhibitions, entertainment, etc.

- Produce an action plan outlining tasks/events, dates and resources.

- Clear the strategy and plan at the highest level within your own company.

- Monitor the implementation plan regularly, adjusting the messages and tactics according to changing circumstances.

Identify your target audiences

For most companies and organisations, target audiences are easily identified; they can include your customers, potential customers, suppliers, workforce, potential employees, investors and shareholders. Sometimes you will want to target just one audience; on other occasions, you may decide to target a number of them and then lastly you may decide that, for very little extra effort, communications with one specific audience might well be of interest to another audience. Your company might have developed a new widget that has taken the market by storm and is obviously of interest to potential customers. However, the news will also be of interest to your workforce and shareholders: after all, they worked to create the success and the shareholders want to see the return on their investment. At the same time, potential employees might be attracted to working for such a successful organisation.

Depending on your messages, your target audiences can be as focused finely to just one person, or it can be wide angled and encompass almost everyone with whom your company or organisation has contact.

Research their current perceptions of your company's product or service

We all like to think our company or organisation is well perceived by the outside world. But what is the reality? Part of a PR practitioner's job is to discover just how a company is perceived. From my own experience, this can be enlightening. Comments from journalists about major FTSE companies have included: 'Oh, yes, we have heard of them, but they don't make contact with us'. 'Oh! Well they generate electricity don't they?' 'It is an interesting company, but I wish they would get in contact'.

The common factor with journalists is that the more you tell them, the more they are likely to be interested in you. After all, they have to fill their news columns and broadcast programmes for every edition.

Similarly, your marketing manager will have done his market research to see how the company's products and services are perceived and the marketing strategy is then based on the results of the research. Like your marketing strategy, you will have to tailor your messages in order to achieve the desired positive reaction from your audiences. Alternatively, you might have to alter the presentation to catch and hold their positive reaction.

Decide on the aim of your communications strategy

Do you want more sales? Do you want more customers? Do you want your share price to be higher? Do you want to be seen as a good employer? Do you want to be seen as environmentally friendly? Do you want to break into new markets? A company may want almost any combination of these, and perhaps a few more. So always keep an eye on the ultimate aim and be prepared to take advantage of the unexpected when it is presented to you.

A Meat and Livestock Commission butcher demonstrates an aspect of meat preparation. The display unit provides a good establishing background; his face can be clearly seen; the meat and the knife make it clear what he is doing; and then the excellent detail, the essential item of safety clothing, a chain mail glove on his left hand.

Decide on the key messages

Always ensure that the key points are included when targeting your audience. These might be relevant benefits, corrections of misconceptions, history of success and innovation, etc. Such comments are likely to be the thread of continuity from one interview to the next.

Identify the means of transmission

At its very simplest, a letter is normally an effective method of communicating with one person. However, you can also communicate through the media, factory visits, exhibitions, leaflets, promotional videos, advertising, faxes, Internet, emails, etc - or a mixture of these channels of communication. All of these have their advantages and perhaps some disadvantages, but the effective communicator will integrate them so that they give each other mutual support.

Decide on the timing to use the various channels to maximum effect

The best analogy for this is sowing the seeds according to plan, so that the whole garden looks its best the day the competition judge comes round. Attending exhibitions, especially the major ones such as Farnborough and the Paris Air Shows, entails about six months' work to plan and execute the supporting PR plan. After all, the stand, chalet, equipment, personnel and other expenses at these huge international exhibitions will cost at least a minimum of £500,000 so the company expects the greatest number of serious and prospective customers to visit the stand and chalet. Even for small to medium enterprises at a smaller, but equally specialised exhibition, where the cost might only be £1,000-£2,000, some well-thought-through PR needs to be properly implemented to make the expenditure on the show well worthwhile.

Three months before the exhibition there should be a press conference to introduce new products, which is aimed at the monthly specialist magazines and specialist writers on the national newspapers so that the target audiences can be well warmed up in advance. Then invitations should be posted to all the known and prospective customers, followed by a media blitz in the few days before the show. During the show itself, try to be in the show's daily magazine in order to maintain interest.

This is a fairly simple résumé of the communications programme to support an exhibition, but it illustrates the necessary co-ordination and integration to ensure success, which would be evidenced by the large numbers of visitors to the stand and chalet already well informed on the products and services. Consequently, there was no need for a briefing on the basics and so the sales teams had an extra 10 minutes' selling time.

Establish what resources are available and required

People, equipment, money for publications, advertising, exhibitions, entertainment, etc.are all in the mix of resources to make PR happen effectively. It does not run on thin air. If you are fully committed to making PR successful, then you or your PR manager will have to decide on the budget, or make sure that he can extract the most effective resources within the limits of the PR budget. In addition, the PR manager must work out his time budget. Is there sufficient time in the 220 working days in a year to do all that is planned?

Produce an action plan

In the course of the year, your action plan has to outline tasks, events, dates and resources. They have to be scheduled and included in the plan must be the availability of senior managers and directors, who ultimately are responsible for PR. Putting across the company message and image successfully is best done by senior personnel.

In your action plan, look at the events you have in your diary, financial results, product launches, exhibitions, advertising campaigns, etc and then create a schedule so that you can have a sustained communications programme with something to publicise every two or three weeks. Each of these events will require their own programme to make sure they happen successfully.

In the Army one always assumes that the best-laid plan seldom survives first contact with the enemy. As a result the Army has an excellent reputation of using its initiative to overcome the unexpected. When I worked with a defence electronics company, I had set up a press briefing on a Thursday for yet another incredibly clever black box of electronics, complete with a guaranteed full house of the key journalists. A couple of days before this carefully planned briefing, I received a call from one of the journalists who apologised that he would not be able to attend as he and the other journalists had been invited to cover an Ariane launch in Guyana on that very day. I then discovered that they would all be back in the UK on the Sunday, so I immediately contacted all the specialists who would be giving the press briefing. I persuaded them to reschedule the briefing to Monday. Before the journalists had left for Guyana, I had told them of the rejigged schedule and as a result I had a full house of journalists which, coincidentally, pleased all the technical staff who had adjusted their busy diaries and found they had a worthwhile audience of influential journalists.

Clear the strategy and plan at the highest level

The ultimate Public Relations Officer within a company or organisation is the Chairman or Chief Executive. So make sure that your strategy and plan have been cleared at the highest level within your own company or group. PR/communications strategy cannot be left entirely to the PR or marketing department. If it is to be fully effective, it is a task for everyone - from the switchboard operator and the factory/warehouse floor workers to the Managing Director. It is therefore absolutely vital that all are made aware of the strategy and the need for it so that everyone communicates the same key messages.

Monitor the execution of the plan regularly

Be prepared to adjust the messages and tactics according to changing circumstances. The most recent and, sadly, the most immediate example of this was in the wake of the World Trade Centre tragedy, when all the airlines had to dramatically alter their planned programmes to take account of the drastic decrease in the number of passengers and the lay-off of staff. They also had to do some hard lobbying to persuade their governments to help them with the increased insurance premiums. All this was an excellent example of monitoring the execution of the plan. Fortunately, most companies are spared the problem of undertaking such a change of tack with their PR programmes. There will probably only be changes in the level of demand for your products and services which might include demand exceeding supply.

Public relations as a marketing tool

The UK Institute of Marketing defines marketing as:

'The management process responsible for identifying, anticipating and satisfying customer requirements profitably'.

PR is part of the marketing mix along with market research, advertising, promotions and the other marketing activities. How you use PR to support marketing will depend on your marketing strategy and the products you wish to market. Pharmaceuticals, food, beauty products and cars will all be marketed differently, but the basics are common to each. These basics of marketing are:

- Market research (identifying potential users, buying motives and habits)

- Market forecasting (predicting future demands and market trends)

- Product planning (deciding product or service range, design, price structure and volume)

- Distribution planning (identifying channels for distribution and sale of product or service to consumer)

- Promotional and sales planning (making contact with potential customers/users and influencing their buying decisions)

- Sales administration

- Public relations

PR is a marketing tool, and is an effective means of reaching target groups. When implementing a marketing strategy, PR is not just there to be used to influence the customer and the potential customer; it can also be used to influence all the target audiences who are interested in your marketing activities. Your market research might throw up interesting and newsworthy results. Perhaps it might discover that women are safer and more considerate drivers and, based on such information, a car manufacturer might be designing cars which are more user-friendly to women. This could well be the basis for a news story which will lay the seed of interest in women drivers who will, you hope, have had their curiosity aroused and be more perceptive to the launch campaign when it happens.

Chapter 9
Press releases

What you'll find in this chapter:

➡ Presentation
➡ Targeting
➡ Content
➡ Timing
➡ Distribution

To ensure your press release does not end up with the other 590 failures, you must make sure it complies to some simple rules. Firstly, it must be about news; newspapers are not interested in marketing gimmicks and self-puffery. Secondly, the leading paragraph should include the five Ws: Who? Why? What? When? and Where?

To assist you in producing a good press release, read the newspapers and trade press for guidance as your piece must be written in journalistic style. It should be instructive, entertaining and well written in order to catch the eye of the news editor who is being continually swamped with information on a wide variety of topics.

The secret to seeing your press release in print is to understand the journalistic process. Their job is to report news and not to edit other people's press releases. If, however, it has been written in the style that they would use, your chances of publication are vastly improved. You must not rehash the last press release you read or wrote but instead focus on the newsworthiness of your particular subject matter. To support it, some of the five Ws should be appropriately included, in order to help focus the mind of the reader to the main point of the story, the news itself.

So what is there in a modern news story that can guide us to writing better and more effective press releases?

The first paragraph should be an exciting summary of the heart of the story, encapsulating its most important and interesting elements. You shouldn't always attempt to tell it all in one sentence, but definitely in the first paragraph. The following paragraphs should elaborate the details, usually in descending order of interest to readers, and, more importantly, have relevance to the key elements of the lead paragraph.

Remember the first reader of your press release is the news editor, and not the publication's readers. If you have not captured the editor's attention with the first sentence, the release is dead and will join the majority of the day's offerings in the bin. Sometimes the headline helps, but do not depend on it. It all hangs on the first sentence, no matter what other nuggets are in the rest of the story.

So model the press release not on other press releases, but on the news in the story itself. A recent story in *The Times* started, 'One in five British children has head lice. So why can't we kill them and why can no one agree how best to tackle them?'

In a couple of terse sentences, the writer has captured the whole story. Even though the five Ws are absent, the introduction makes it almost impossible for the reader not to read the whole story, and yes, it really was interesting! So how does this compare with the more typical press release? 'John Smith, Chairman of ABC plc, announced today that two new directors have been appointed.'

Would you want to read further or is it another prime candidate for the bin? Who is John Smith? What is ABC plc and why should this be of interest to anyone outside the company and why should any outsiders care? It might be quite a nice ego boost for the two new directors, but where is the news in this?

Let's try again and this time aim to grab the news editor's attention: 'Up-to-date international taxation management and patent law skills will boost ABC plc's export capabilities as a result of two new directors being appointed to the Board, it was announced today by the company's Chairman, John Smith'.

This slightly long sentence tells the news editor that something newsworthy has happened. There is every good chance that he will want to read further to see all the five Ws in action. Who are they? Why will they be effective? What have they to offer? When will they start? How will the company be served better? etc.

It's worthwhile reading some of your target press just to see how they define news and how they present it. They all have their slightly different styles and sometimes it might be more effective if you produce a couple of different versions of the press release to meet the demands of the different media. Do it properly and you will be able to produce an exciting story from something which could well be perceived as routine and mundane by the company itself; but do not go over the top. This is why reading a publication to assess its definition of news is vital.

Recently, I had persuaded a major regional evening newspaper to look at a technology story based on a new blue screen technology fabric for virtual TV and video studios. A couple of weeks earlier I had had another technology story in the same paper, so I had a good idea of exactly what was wanted. I drafted a press release for clearance by the client. Back it came. What had been a press release concentrating on the product itself was now a confused mess of other issues and concerns. Sure, they were of vital interest to the client company, but they detracted from the news of the story for the journalist concerned. The client company and I then had a discussion on how to present it. Eventually we agreed to trim off all the superfluous concerns and issues and to concentrate on the technology and its benefits. Much to the client's delight, the story was carried verbatim, complete with a photograph.

At the end of the day, the press release writer proposes, but the editor disposes. Just make sure your writing skills reflect contemporary techniques and not the ones of recent history.

Press release checklist

Presentation is just as important as the writing and content of the press release - it must have eye appeal. To get some tips on how to make the layout most effective, take a look at the newspapers' front pages and see which one grabs your attention. They are designed specifically to catch the casual sales reader (usually five per cent of their readership) who will make a purchase based on the eye-catching front cover, rather than the 95 per cent who are regular readers.

With regard to press releases, the proportion of regular to casual readership is the opposite to newspapers as those from government departments, the police and local government offices tend to be always read, but not necessarily used. The other 95 per cent have to have visual appeal as well as good copy. Lay out on the floor of your office a selection of press releases and look down at them. Fairly rapidly you will see the ones that say 'read me'.

The hallmarks to success with regard to real eye appeal and readability are in the following checklist. Remember:

1. Newspapers, magazines, television and radio stations are bombarded with news releases. Four out of five releases end up in waste paper bins, some after no more than a cursory glance. To avoid a similar fate for your efforts:

    •   Ensure that your topic or event warrants a release;

- Lay it out professionally;

- Target it properly.

2. A relevant, well presented release sent to the right media outlet could be used and is a cost-effective way of getting your messages across. But however interesting the message, a poorly presented release sent to the wrong outlet will be binned. Don't shoot first and call what you hit the target.

3. Ask yourself:

- Does the subject warrant a release?

- What am I trying to achieve from it and what points do I want to get across?

- What should the distribution be?

- Is it worth arranging a press facility?

- Should I clear my proposals with other interested parties?

Presentation

4. Use headed, white A4-sized release paper identifying your organisation. A coloured motif alongside the organisation's name can be eye-catching and effective. Do not use coloured paper and do not have any vertically laid out print.

5. Use a professional layout including:

- A straightforward catchline in capitals;

- Double-spaced typing (no underlining);

- Short sentences, short paragraphs;

- No jargon or abbreviations;

- First names, not initials;

- One sheet of paper, or at most two (if it runs to more than one page put 'more' or 'm/f' (more follows) at the bottom of the first sheet and 'end' at the bottom of the final sheet);

- One side of the paper only;

- Good, wide margins, at least one inch (to allow for the sub-editor's notes).

6. It must have (at top or bottom) the name and address of the issuing office, a reference number (e.g. No.01/98), the date, and a manned telephone number, extension and preferably the name of the person able to answer questions about the release and arrange media facilities. This creates the impression that your company is media-friendly, as you are volunteering to be constantly available to the press.

Targeting

7. There is no point in sending a release about a Leeds Royal visit to a newspaper in Hampshire, or one on defence equipment to a beekeepers' magazine. Use a good media reference book, such as Benn's, to target your release accurately.

Content

8. Ensure that your release answers the five Ws; Who, What, Where, Why and When, as well as How. The opening paragraph must put over the main points (e.g. Pop star Madonna will name the new dog biscuit when she visits Smith's Pet Foods' Leeds factory for its centenary celebrations).

   In this case the When and How can come later.

9. Remember KISS - Keep It Simple, Stupid.

   Keep it short, make it lively; but don't try to out-write Ernest Hemingway. Supply the facts, clearly and simply, and leave the journalists to do their job. Releases that go to rival newsrooms are almost invariably rewritten anyway.

10. Each sentence should be short - around 20 words. Do you ever see long sentences in newspapers? The whole release should be kept under 300 words. The main points must be given in the opening paragraphs, followed by explanatory material in descending order of importance. Sub-editors tend to cut from the bottom.

11. Avoid business jargon; it might be comprehensible to you, but not to the journalist looking at dozens of releases every day.

12. Include all appropriate local angles - the provincial media is usually extremely parochial in outlook, e.g. Winsford reflective ink company, Cardiff-born Sales Director, etc.

13. A short quotation from the Managing Director or other relevant person should be used if it adds to the story. Never say such obvious comments as 'We are pleased that we have succeeded'. It is much better and more interesting to say, 'We won the order against stiff

opposition from five competitors, but it was the speed of our planned delivery that impressed the client'.

14. Do explain briefly what the company does (e.g. Britain's largest and oldest pet food firm, with processing plants in Leeds, Swansea and Edinburgh). Whatever the angle of the particular release, it is a useful vehicle for such key points. However, your releases should be about matters of genuine public interest. News editors can easily spot a blatant attempt to get a free puff for a company or product and most such plugs end up in the bin.

15. At the end of every press release have your boilerplate paragraph which is always there to remind the reader just exactly what your company or organisation does. It gives you an opportunity to put your company in perspective and as editors see many press releases daily, they tend not to object to boilerplates as a gentle reminder of your company. Sometimes the boilerplate will be included in the news story, and that is a great bonus. It is most likely to happen in the trade and technical magazines, especially on slow news days.

16. Ensure your release is 100 per cent accurate.

17. Take care not to breach security, commercial confidentiality or stock market rules.

18. Headlines should be simple and straightforward. Try not to use jokey, eye-catching headlines. That is the job of the journalist.

Facility notices

19. If a facility for the media is associated with the news release, add a facility note. It should say that they are invited to attend the event at (place) at (time) on (date). Briefly explain what is on offer and give directions on how to get there. Enclose an acceptance form or invite them to ring you to let you know if they will be attending - you will need to know who is coming so that you can brief your company and make hospitality arrangements.

20. If you are inviting the press to attend an event, make sure it is at a convenient time for them and not necessarily for you.

Timing

21. Time your release for maximum impact. Announce a new contract when there is no major news story dominating the headlines, which will likely wipe out much of the lesser news.

22. Give plenty of warning of a VIP visit, factory opening or similar event. Normally two weeks is about right to allow the media to arrange coverage, although of course when a major news story breaks they will drop everything and turn up at no notice.

When organising a Royal visit, do make sure you have a choice of locations from where photographers and camera operators can have a clear view of the Royal visitor.

Embargoes

23. A release is usually intended for use as soon as it is issued, so the phrase 'for immediate release' is superfluous. However, if there are good reasons (such as the publication of a weighty report that requires study), it may be issued under embargo.

24. This should be made clear at the top of the release, e.g.

'EMBARGOED UNTIL 0001 HOURS GMT 27 NOVEMBER 2002

This information is sent to you for your convenience in advance of publication of the Blank Report. It is not for publication, broadcast or use on club tapes before 00.01 GMT on Friday, 27 November'.

Club tapes are found in public places, such as clubs, which have publicly accessible news agency material. Originally on printed paper, but nowadays it really relates to any media, including the Internet, where information can be publicly available.

25. Use embargoes very sparingly: they are sometimes broken - usually by accident - and can cause problems. Never use the system merely for your own convenience.

Please see an example of an original press release on pages 61-2.

Press Release
14/00

3 July 2000

Reflec Wins £500,000 Micro-Grinding Contract

Reflec plc, the Winsford based reflectives and micro-grinding company, has won its first long-term micro-grinding contract worth approximately £500,000. Over the next 12 months Reflec will grind several thousand tonnes of special salt to two figure micron size particles for a major supplier of solutions to the oil industry. This salt solution is used as a temporary plug for oil wells, with the solution crystallising to form a solid plug, and then by injecting steam into the plug the salt dissolves reopening the well and the solution disperses into the sea water.

The contract was awarded to Reflec because of its capability to micro-grind salt to meet the client's very tight tolerances. The specified particle size ensures the optimum dispersion of salt into the solution, technically known as completion fluid. In addition, Reflec has proved it can deliver consistent quality from batch to batch.

With the client requiring just in time (JIT) deliveries, Reflec will be turning round typical orders of 150 tonnes in three days. This contract will ensure that one of Reflec's processing plants will be fully utilised for about a third of the year undertaking ambient grinding that delivers good margins.

m/f

Commenting on this contract, Nick Rowbottom, Reflec's Operations Director, said, 'This contract confirms our capability to process materials that meet tightly defined specifications. There are benefits for both our client and Reflec. Our client has a guaranteed supply of micro-ground salt at a pre-determined cost and Reflec benefits from regular work with good profitable returns. We hope to confirm more long-term contracts in the near future'.

Reflec plc has three divisions. The process division, PlastChem Ltd, specialises in cryogenic and ambient grinding for industry, for its own reflective inks and its anti-corrosion coatings. The reflective division, Reflective Technologies International Ltd, is one of the world's major producers of reflective inks and its inks are currently exported to Australia, the Far East, Europe and the USA where they are largely used by the textile and fashion trade. The coatings division produces Kelvar anti-corrosion coatings which are used in the protection of metal components in aggressive environments. Kelvar is in use in the Far East and the UK on oil platforms, mass transit railways and power stations. Reflec's website is www.reflec.co.uk. The company employs 42 people and is based at Winsford, Cheshire.

end

For further information please contact:
Ian Proud
Franklin Associates
Tel: 020 7831 9421

Reflec plc, Road One, Winsford Industrial Estate, Winsford, Cheshire CW7 3QQ
Tel 01606 593 911 Fax 01606 559 535
www.reflec.co.uk   email info@reflec.co.uk

Distribution

Your press releases must be sent to those media that are going to be interested in it. Your checklist for this is likely to be:

- the local media, including TV and radio

- the local news agencies

- the specialist trade and technical press

- the regional business magazines

- the city and financial press

- the overseas press, especially if you have a good export order

When you send out your press release, it is in your best interest to find out how the journalist likes to receive it. Some journalists are so bombed out with emails, for example, that they are deleted almost as fast as they arrive. In this instance, they prefer hard copy which they can read, so send a fax. However, there are others, especially the writers on the trade and technical magazines, who like to receive them in email form. If it is well written, they can then edit it on screen and have it ready for inclusion in the publication almost immediately.

Of course, there is also the option of sending it by post. This is normally fine for many of the monthly trade and technical magazines and the regular weekly columns in newspapers, such as the appointments and other weekly features.

Once you have sent the press release, it is worthwhile phoning the journalist to see if it has been received. It probably has, but has it been overwhelmed by all the other press releases? Do not become exasperated if the journalist says it has not arrived, merely offer to resend it. This normally ensures that it is then read.

Arranging the right picture

1. The best way of finding out what sort of photographs newspapers and magazines are likely to use is to read the publications regularly. You should maintain a stock of pictures for publicity use, featuring the main products and company personalities.

2. For newspapers, 5 inch x 7 inch colour pictures are normally sufficient. For television and some magazines, colour is required - either colour prints or 35 mm transparencies are

Two senior personnel at Cranfield College of Aeronautics. Despite being in the open, a good position was pre-planned for this photo, with not only the college name providing the establishing background, but a plane helps to reinforce the image.

acceptable for TV stations. Remember, a TV screen is in landscape format so do not send TV stations portrait format pictures. Increasingly, print media will accept colour prints or download photos from a website.

3. You should have in your possession pictures of the main products, both static and in use, preferably being operated by people. There are specialist magazines that will be happy to publish pictures of new equipment on its own, including close-ups of what, to the expert, are its interesting features. But the general press prefers to include people.

4. If you are initiating a picture story, you may well be able to interest the media themselves in covering it. If not, obtain the services of a good photographer and brief him carefully on the aim. Always look for unusual angles, e.g. using a crane or forklift as a camera platform.

5. Avoid stilted, staged shots. They will be 'binned'. But do not trivialise. Many would regard a picture of a topless model lolling over a piece of company equipment as inappropriate.

6. If you have persuaded the media to cover the story themselves, make sure the background is suitable, the equipment is being operated correctly and the people involved are properly dressed in the appropriate safety kit. Get rid of any bottles, glasses, cigarettes, explicit pin-ups or other inappropriate objects that might mar the picture.

7. If you are providing the media with pictures, they must be clearly captioned. Always give names (including first names) from left to right. Include brief titles or job descriptions (e.g. Managing Director or factory foreman), the name and role of the equipment shown, the name and location of the company or establishment where the action has taken place, and the date, where relevant. The caption must be attached to the photograph so it can be read whilst looking at the photograph, i.e. just as a reader sees the picture and caption in print. Do not attach the caption copy to the back of the photograph. It is awkward for the recipient in the newsroom and as a result, has an increased chance of being binned.

8. Keep the number of words down to a minimum.

Chapter 10
Press conferences

What you'll find in this chapter:

➠ Handling a press conference
➠ Examples of how to relate to the media
➠ Organising media facilities

Before arranging a press conference, first ask yourself whether it is really necessary and will it be more effective than a press release. In the same way as press releases end up in the bin, press conferences too can have a similar fate as they tend to be poorly attended and even more meanly reported. You must have something stunningly important to absorb a journalist's time, so go over the simple checklist:

• What is there that cannot be said in press releases?

• Will outsiders consider your news as important or even more important than the other issues of the day?

• Do you want to be asked probing questions?

• Don't you have other opportunities to speak to the media?

There are two types of press conferences which companies undertake. Firstly, there is the planned press conference where a company believes it has something important to announce, and secondly, there is the instant press conference normally held at very short notice where the company or organisation has to deal with an emergency, dispute or some other unwelcome event.

Here is an example of a planned press conference I organised some years ago. It was held at Gatwick Airport for a party of Royal Engineers returning from a tour of duty in Pakistan, just over the border from Afghanistan, where (before the current military action) they had been teaching Afghanis how to find, identify and neutralise land mines, many millions of which were scattered over the country. To liven it up, I went to the Royal School of Military Engineering and borrowed a dozen defused, safe mines of the type commonly found in Afghanistan. When I returned, I gave the Royal Engineers a briefing on the press and the questions which were likely to be asked. The mines gave the photographers some immediate establishing material and the officer in charge could pick up the various mines and explain in some gory detail what injuries they could inflict. As a result, the press conference went well.

There was an occasion when I had to hold an impromptu press conference as a Plessey executive, who had been held hostage in Libya, was suddenly released and flown back to the UK. There was intense press interest in his release and at short notice we decided that it would be best if the press could meet him on arrival in the country so we could have some control over what he said. The press was informed, which was no big deal, as they had done their homework and knew he was returning soon. When he arrived at the airport we had a room booked for the press conference, we met him as soon as he came through immigration, had a quick briefing with him and led him into the press conference. There must have been two dozen people there. We let him say his set piece, and answer about six questions before whisking him away to some peace and quiet. By doing this, we saved the press from going round and round in circles with the same questions, and they had the story, embellished with a quotation or two from the executive. As it was late afternoon, we also wanted them to have plenty of time to file their copy.

Handling a press conference

The way in which a press conference is handled may have far-reaching results. Ways to create an interesting and well delivered presentation are as follows:

- Be straightforward and truthful.

- Timing is important. Complete your press conference by 11.30 am and you have the best chance of having it covered in reasonable depth. There may be occasions when, for legal or operational reasons, it has to be later. If you cannot complete it by 4.30 pm, either put out a press release or delay it until the next day. If the next day is Friday, it is definitely a press release job. Press conferences on Fridays end up in the Saturday newspapers and the reader's reaction is not as significant as it would be on a normal weekday.

- Everything said is 'on the record'.

At presentations and press conferences, make sure the backdrop is not only branded, but also done in such a way that no amount of editing by the photo editor can cut it out.

- Make sure that the main point of the press conference is newsworthy.

- Be prepared to give some background information (again on the record) for reporters so they can put the news in perspective.

- Some journalists may not be specialists in the subject being announced at the press conference, so take care to explain everything simply and clearly. Take time. If the press conference is hurried, some important points might be missed; one correspondent who misses an important point may be missing it for millions of readers, viewers and listeners.

- If complicated figures are involved or there are extracts from official documents, copies of this material should be made available to correspondents. It saves their shorthand and they can concentrate on the actualities of the event.

- Leave plenty of time for questions.

- Make a video recording of the press conference for post mortems and lessons learned.

- Make sure you have a good press pack for the journalists available before the press conference starts, which must include extracts from the main speech. This saves journalists using their rusty shorthand; they can then concentrate on the speech, highlighting the parts they want to ask questions on and it ensures the key points you want to put across are not missed.

An unsuccessful press conference

Here is an example of how <u>not</u> to describe a takeover to the press:

'I won't apologise for being late because I was at a crucial meeting which delayed me. I'm an accountant and hate publicity. To be honest, I have more important things to do than speak to journalists who make up stories for a living.

Now which paper do you represent? The *Financial Times*! An excellent paper. And you? The *Daily Mail*! I think you'll be wasting your time here as we won't be discussing women's issues today. The presence of the FT is quite sufficient as it's the only paper the business world reads.

This is my first press conference and I really do believe that it is a futile exercise. However, I will still go on and discuss what our company is doing now that the takeover is complete but I do warn you that if any of you misquote me, I will immediately contact our lawyers.

The takeover was pretty routine. The integration of new companies has always been a problem. When we took over XYZ plc, we found all their factories to be in a bad way, with chemical pollution rampant, suppliers unpaid, the supporting infrastructure almost non-existent and the local unions causing havoc with our labour relations.

Much to my surprise, we have sorted out these problems. We have fixed the leaking factories, repaired the pollution control systems, settled the outstanding invoices of most local suppliers, restored water and electricity and the workforce is now back at work. This is all due to the damn good work of our head office staff from London.

I am not going to give details of the chemical pollution as it will only attract the attention of Greenpeace, or how we restored the water and electricity as that is commercially confidential information. I am also not willing to tell you what suppliers are left unpaid and how we resolved the local union problem.

To be honest, I'd prefer it if you didn't write anything at all about these matters. I've got to get back to work so you have three minutes remaining of my time.

In answer to your request for me to talk about the takeover team, please write in your newspapers that they have done extremely well. It will be good for their morale if they see that in print!

So you have been talking to out Scottish lawyers and have been informed that they assisted us in sorting out the mess? That's typical of you hacks to snoop around digging up useless tittle-tattle! If you mention them, I will have the Press Council onto you. For your information, the Scottish lawyers had nothing to do with it, only head office.

Are you so unprepared that you want to use our phone lines to file copy? And you want a tour of our acquired factories to take some pictures? This is not possible. You will have to just take a picture of me as I do not have the time to chauffeur you from place to place'.

Reports files by journalists

To Press Association

'British company has successfully taken over XYZ plc's facilities in this country. Suggest strong protest to the Chief Executive as his director here is not co-operating with the press, has an attitude problem and refuses to provide us with facilities. Regrettably, it is impossible to get any worthwhile news from him'.

To Scottish newspapers

'Do not expect news from here. There is strong anti-Scottish bias from top management. Am returning home'.

A letter of complaint to an editor ends up being used in a critical editorial.

Press summary

'The local press report in depth on the hostile takeover of XYZ plc. Chemical pollution has worsened, XYZ's factories have not had their water and electricity restored, the local suppliers have been short-changed with their outstanding invoices, the unions have been bribed, the workforce fear an asset stripping operation and the takeover company's lawyers are ill qualified for the job.

The Scottish press have editorials criticising the use of Scottish lawyers and the Press Council has sent a strong complaint to the company's Chairman'.

A successful press conference

'Sorry to have kept you waiting, and I'm delighted so many of you could attend. I see you have had some coffee.

The takeover of XYZ plc's factories in this country has been successfully completed. We are now in the process of integrating them into our newly enlarged company. There is some excellent synergy; the factories have some excellent potential and some good suppliers.

When we moved our people into the town we discovered the factories in a deplorable state of repair and that was affecting the production; it ruined the morale of the workforce, 30 per cent of whom were temporarily laid off.

Our first priority was to weatherproof the factories and I'm delighted to say a couple of German companies in the region did an absolutely first-class job in very quick time. The factories were weatherproofed sufficiently for the production facilities to be overhauled and then swung into full production, ensuring that we could use the whole of the workforce to full effect.

Before we took over, a major problem which had resulted from the poor maintenance was that the pollution control systems were totally useless. Unrefined chemicals from the factories and the associated storage plants were leaking in alarming quantities into the local waterways. The main pollutants were cleaning fluids - the sort of stuff that gives the rivers that soap suds effect - light lubricating oils and silver nitrate. The cleaning fluids are about as dangerous as the domestic washing-up liquid most of you have in your kitchens and its main danger to river life is that undiluted it can suffocate fish and other life; but if diluted, fish and other river life probably will be cleaner than they have ever been before. The light lubricating oil is slightly more serious: it does the normal things that oil in water does, but as it is very light it evaporates eventually; it has caused some damage to river life, but it will quickly recover. The quantities of silver nitrate are, by comparison, small and when diluted, non-toxic. However, the economic loss of such valuable chemicals, which we can recycle and reuse, impacts on the running costs of these factories.

We also have persuaded the local authorities to sort out the infrastructure, water, electricity, etc and as a result not only do our new factories have water, but also many of the people who live in the town have benefited and we like to think this is our contribution to good community relations.

As you can well imagine, the trade unions have been trying to impose unrealistic working practices now the factories are back up and running. Fortunately our Scottish law specialists have been able to make sure the proper legalities are observed. They were absolutely vital in making sure that this takeover and the factories resuming production happened quickly and efficiently.

Although we did not have to pay the outstanding invoices of suppliers dated before the takeover, we have done so. The sums involved were fairly modest, but it has helped the local economy and will help us develop our newly acquired business.

If you want to give any credit to the success of this takeover, I would suggest that you give credit to our Scottish lawyers. The other good story is the rapid way in which we dealt with the pollution problems. We had the services of a brilliant team of Canadian environmental engineers.

The factories now have a great future within our company, the future of the workforce has been stabilised and we look forward to them making a positive contribution in the near future.

I'm sorry about the lack of telephones in the area, but if you want to file copy we have a couple of mobile phones you can use.

I beg your pardon! You haven't been to the factory. Please see my colleague here and we'll drive you there.

Thank you for coming to this press conference. Press packs with all our contact numbers are available for you at the back of the room and if you have any further questions we'll be pleased to help you'.

Here follows the press' reaction to the meeting:

Press summary

'XYZ plc has now successfully integrated into its parent company. The Chief Executive has managed the takeover and has had XYZ's factories repaired, labour disputes resolved and local infrastructure fixed. Seen to be sympathetic to local concerns, especially pollution. 'A great future within our company'. 'The future of the workforce has been stabilised'. 'We look forward to these factories making a positive contribution in the near future'.

The possible consequences of such a presentation are numerous:

- The agencies and newspapers file copious copy. Personality stories appear in the national, local, trade and technical press on the people involved in the legal and

environmental engineering aspects of the takeover. The Scottish press emphasise the professionalism of the company's Scottish lawyers in resolving many problems.

- The German press report on the success of the German companies in carrying out first aid building works on the acquired factories.

- The Canadian press give equally good coverage of the Canadian companies that solved the pollution control problems with the acquired factories.

- TV news coverage looks at the televisual aspects of the factories; pollution before and after; the tatty factories before and after; as well as 30 seconds of the Chief Executive at the press conference.

- In addition to the straight news coverage, with plenty of advice to invest in the company, most of the opinion columns in all the heavies praise the management style of the Chief Executive.

At all times be co-operative: apologise for any delays that may have occurred, let the press use the company's phone lines to ring their papers and always assist them in taking a picture of the establishment. Should the journalists sense any kind of hostility or apathy, the backlash could be enormous, resulting in a great deal of critical press.

Organising media facilities

Successful press conferences and media facilities only happen as a result of careful planning, double-checking and rehearsal. This aide memoire gives you a quick checklist for success in organising press facilities and TV visits.

1. **Before you start:**

   - Identify the reason for the press conference facility.

   - Evaluate your message.

   - Assess press interest.

2. **Anticipate:**

   - Media requirements.

   - In-house manpower and support.

3. **Contact** (through news release or by telephone):

   - News Editors.

   - Picture Editors.

The original *African Queen* was the star of one of the London Boat Shows. An early morning press opportunity to film and photograph her on the Thames resulted in extensive coverage. Similar photos to this were published and this particular one was reproduced by the owner as a postcard to sell in his Key Largo Hotel, where the boat is based.

- Specialist correspondents.

4. **Timing**:

- Preferably mid-morning.
- Preferably early in the week; NEVER Friday and preferably not Monday.

5. **Preparation**:

- Totally thorough.
- Think, rehearse, then think again!

6. **Press pack:**

    *   Better too much than too little.

    *   Make the contents easy to read and assimilate.

    *   Help the press through the pack by indexing.

7. **On the day:**

    *   Check and double-check - the helpers, the interviewees, the photographic platform, the wet weather programme, the phones, etc.

    *   Think of what YOU would like to have available if you were the reporter, correspondent or cameraman covering the event.

    *   Stick to your schedule.

Finally, be positive!

Chapter 11
Your public face

Who is your public face? Is it the Chief Executive, the MD, Finance Director, or even your PR manager? Whoever it is, it must be the member of staff who is responsible for the public image of your company. The best person is normally the Chief Executive or Chairman. After all, the buck stops with them and they are responsible for everything, including PR and corporate communications. News organisations are wary in interviewing the PR manager or PR adviser. They know that although PR executives may be very knowledgeable about the company, they are there to advise on presentation of company information. So reporters much prefer to interview a senior manager or director who was involved in the decision making process. However, do use your PR manager or adviser to advise you on how best to present yourself and your company in public, much in the same way as you would use your personnel manager or company secretary to advise you on their areas of responsibility.

Used properly, good corporate communications can positively raise your profile in your market place, community and elsewhere. As a result, it is vital that your PR manager is viewed as an important member of the company and is at the heart of all its proceedings.

I was once part of a PR team who were corporate communications advisers to a small AIM (Alternative Investment Market) listed company based in Cheshire. We were invited to attend all the management meetings, so we were fully informed and better able to advise the company on how to present itself to its target audiences. As a result of this, many outside organisations knew we competently reflected the company's views, policy, successes and strategy and they came to us for answers and guidance. However, do note that it is always a director or senior manager of the company who is the public face of the company, not the external advisers.

What qualities should you look for in a corporate communicator if you want to improve the corporate communications service of your company or organisation? Many companies employ a journalist, as he is able to use the tricks of his trade to ensure press coverage. Others might prefer to hire an experienced, qualified PR manager, or if the company is small, select a manager who is willing to learn on the job and make time for this important role. Often the best person in a small company is the marketing or sales manager. Such a person is usually extrovert and believes in the business as a successful deliverer of products and services. He is also likely to be able to explain the company to its external audiences in simple English.

Terms of reference for your corporate communicator

To do his job effectively, your corporate communicator will be responsible for a number of communication activities. By the time you look at the list you might wonder how he will be able to do his day job, but a carefully chosen individual should have a natural enthusiasm which means that he can gain willing support from other company staff. The following list of responsibilities is fairly comprehensive but not every company will want everything, so do tailor the list to suit:

- Advice on presentation of policy
- Event management
- Exhibitions
- Financial PR
- House magazines
- Letters to the public, press and shareholders
- Media relations
- Newsletters
- Speechwriting

- Sponsorship

- Website management

His areas of responsibility are dependent on the level of support the company can provide. A company must treat him as follows:

- He must be kept fully informed, with immediate access to top managers and directors, so that he knows the background to key decisions.

- Give him time to learn the job, develop his media contacts and attend a media or corporate communications course.

- Let him use his initiative in order to deal with problems and press interest, especially when there is little or no time to seek clearance.

- Give him guidance on the presentation of policy, but do not set it out in black and white.

- Do not have an inquest every time something slightly critical appears in the press. Take an overall view that the main messages are being transmitted clearly in the media.

- Give him a title that reflects his importance in your company, and emphasise it to insiders and outsiders, so that the media will consider him as their first point of contact.

- Give him a budget.

Your corporate communicator should have a title, not just to give him a place in the internal hierarchy, but to reflect his importance in the organisation. In industry and commerce, your corporate communicator should have the confidence of all, no matter what his place in the company.

So, you have identified and appointed your corporate communicator. What can you now expect from him?

- Let him make his contacts with the local, trade and technical press and learn the media's modus operandi.

- Once he has become acquainted with the main aspects of the job, he should be able to judge when the company can communicate with the press.

- An integral part of his job will be to monitor the press and the broadcast media, to see just how the press is reporting business and technical news. He should then be better able to exploit unscheduled opportunities to promote the company in the press.

- He should be capable of advising on the presentation of policy, perhaps sometimes recommending that certain subjects should not be publicised.

- He should be able to write speeches for the Chairman and Chief Executive, and on occasions deliver speeches himself.

- He should have responsibility for drafting replies to shareholders and the press to be signed off by the Chairman.

Some of the corporate communicator's responsibilities are fairly self-explanatory, but some can be better used if looked at in more detail.

'Aha! One of my press releases actually made it.' The author, as the Joint Services Public Relations Officer in Malta, doing his daily check of the local media.

Newsletters

These are normally a marketing tool, with reports of sales and technical successes, all designed to catch the attention of existing and potential customers. Once you decide to produce newsletters, you must maintain the momentum. The minimum should be three a year, a good average is four, and if you feel you are producing sufficient material, you could produce six. Maintain a consistent house style, have a good number of pictures, emphasise customer satisfaction and be prepared for it to be seen by a far wider audience than you might expect. Have copies on display in your reception area, make sure all the necessary people in the company have copies, encourage company employees to submit their own copy, and finally, give them their own by-line on the story.

House magazines

The aim of a house magazine is to keep the staff informed of activities in the company as well as a certain amount of parish pump gossip, births, marriages, retirements, hobbies, external successes, etc. The level of complexity will depend on budget, collection of news and writing skills. Ultimately, the house magazine gives the company a means of providing some extra glue which holds the company together. Its frequency of publication will be dependent on a number of obvious factors, but like newsletters, three a year is a minimum and the economic maximum is 12.

Whatever the size, house magazines can really succeed if the staff willingly and enthusiastically contribute. One highly successful house magazine was just for the corporate head office staff at a major plc. The Chief Executive's secretary produced it and it was very well written. At the other end of the scale, at Ocean Group plc, I was responsible for the company's house newspaper, six editions annually, with contributions from all over the world. It circulated to all the company's 11,000 staff and its pensioners. With such a worldwide circulation, parish pump gossip was kept to a minimum, as the aim was to let everyone know what was happening in the company's 450 sites across 42 countries. However, I also used the magazine, *Ocean News*, as an extra means of communication with other target audiences, the press, the financial community and analysts. It enabled me to inform these key external audiences just how the company made its money at the coalface. Because of the importance the company attached to the house magazine, the Chief Executive cleared all items of corporate interest.

A house magazine is for internal communications with the workforce and that really is a personnel departmental function. So you should consider including the house magazine in the personnel department's budget, even though the corporate communicator will produce it.

News on developments and successes within a company or organisation must be told to the workforce first and to the outside world, including the press, second. Megaphone management is disastrous and will very rapidly demoralise your workforce and your customers' confidence will be lost.

On one occasion when I was working at Ocean Group, I took a call from a national newspaper asking for confirmation that the company was rationalising its workforce with 1,200 redundancies, as reported by PA. Trying hard to sound as if I were not totally surprised, I replied that I would check it out and phone back. I was immediately on the phone to my main Board Director boss. He was equally mystified. Moments later the Chief Executive was in my doorway apologising for letting the news slip out in the course of conversation with one of PA's business correspondents. With the Personnel Director leading, the company then instituted an immediate communications programme to tell the worldwide workforce as soon as possible about the redundancy programme. Without any prompting the Chief Executive led the communications programme and he personally went to every office where there were to be redundancies and he told everyone there what was being done and why he was doing it. 'I made the decision and therefore it is only right I should tell you personally and take your questions,' he prefaced every meeting.

By taking control, by being seen to be the man in charge of the redundancy programme and then telling company staff personally, he regained the upper ground. Whilst he was not necessarily liked for what he did, he most certainly gained the respect of his staff for taking full responsibility. Naturally the redundancy programme was subject to a full internal communications programme, including using the house magazine.

Many house magazine editors make sure that they include news stories which they hope will be picked up by the newspaper correspondents who receive it. Regrettably, there are some house magazine editors and corporate communicators who miss the opportunity to use this channel of communication with the press. The great advantage of doing this is that the stories will be written in a news feature style, without being restrained by the limits of space of a normal press release. As a result, it will be a much fuller report, and the newspaper reporter will be in a better position to lift the complete story and use it.

Speechwriting

This is a golden opportunity for your corporate communicator to connect with the local community. Organisations such as the Round Table, the Rotary Club, schools, etc. are always looking for people to orate. Speeches at local events are seen as a source of copy for the local media.

Providing your corporate communicator follows a few simple rules you will create an excellent line of communication to your community:

Perfect your style and suit the speech to your audience

Your audience is there to be stimulated and their interest aroused. Reading from a set script is an immediate turn-off. It is much better that you have a handful of cards with the key points written down, as you will sound much more relaxed. If you want to be really confident, practise your speech beforehand against a stopwatch. A couple of good practice runs and you will have learned your lines almost word perfect and your cards will be there just as a reminder.

At one major PLC, the directors were practising speeches for a presentation. One director was fully conversant with his subsidiary and up he went to the lectern, pulled out his script and then started to read out the speech in a very boring monotone. After a couple of minutes of very turgid delivery, I asked him to stop. 'You have the best company of its type in the world and you really know the business. Listening to you does not reflect reality. Do me a favour, put your script to one side and let's start again'. He did so and immediately conveyed the interest, verve and confidence that made everyone really believe he was the bees' knees in the offshore oil industry.

Being lucid, clear and enthusiastic are what audiences appreciate and will make speechwriting easier. Jokes can add to the appeal of the speech, but use them wittily and make sure that the audience are in the mood. Do ensure that you make eye-to-eye contact, speak loudly and slowly, vary the pitch of your speech and enunciate. It is also important to dress smartly and be upright in your posture at all times.

If you are writing a speech for your Chairman or Chief Executive, try to write in the style that suits their own personal style of delivery. If you have the opportunity to use audio visual aids, check them carefully beforehand. Fortunately, in these days of PowerPoint presentations from laptops you are not likely to be embarrassed by 35 mm slides jamming, being projected upside down, etc. Again, ensure the slides match the presenter's style of delivery and provide the speech in time for him to rehearse and amend as he wishes.

A couple of years ago, I was in a meeting with the Chief Executive of a small AIM listed company and his brokers. They were advising him on a fundraising exercise. At this meeting the Chief Executive was going through the presentation which had been drafted by the brokers. My client, the Chief Executive, stumbled his way through the presentation and finally at slide 17, he reached the point of his speech. It was at this moment that I interrupted: 'Peter, stop and give me that and I'll redo the presentation'.

Next day, I had totally rewritten the presentation, in a style that suited his style of delivery and the reason for the fundraising was right up front on slide three. Off he went on the fundraising trail looking for £4 million and some other two dozen companies looking for funds simultaneously. He ended up with £7.25 million because the various fund managers were impressed with his style and confidence. Much of that was due to having the presentation which matched his personality.

Make only a few points

Keep the key points you want to four or five. Do not laboriously plough through every point that you think you need to say. It makes for a turgid address, no invitations for more speeches and the local press will be quickly turned off. If you do have something controversial to say and what to argue to gain support, then it is quite effective to repeat it twice. The audience then is absolutely clear that this a major part of your speech.

Whilst arranging your material, review your condensed ideas and weigh their relative importance to your total requirements. By doing this, you will be able to divide the subject into self-contained sections. Head each section and use these headings to form a framework of the main talk. Do make sure that you have a positive and forceful introduction and conclusion.

Stand by with some extra material should someone else use most of your speech material. The neatest use of Plan B I have seen was when, after an Army dinner, the first speaker used nearly all the guest speaker's material. Being a quick thinker, the guest speaker grabbed his menu and made a few quick scribbles on his hand and delivered a totally impromptu speech based on the dishes on the menu. It brought the house down and being very diplomatic, he did not complain to the host or the speaker who tried to eclipse him. What did happen was that he found himself very popular and was invited to do more speeches, not just because he was witty, but because he could make a good speech.

Do not speak ad infinitum

Do not continue after 15 minutes, or if pushed, let 20 be your very maximum. Not only is there the problem of the audience's attention span, but many of these meetings have a time limit.

If the press are likely to be there, have copies of the speech available to hand out. Print them as a press release and entitle it, 'Extracts from the Speech on ---- by-' and make sure the print is double-spaced. You will make friends with journalists if you hand out copies of the speech beforehand but do put in brackets 'Check against delivery'. The journalists will save their shorthand, can absorb the details more efficiently and will be in a position to ask sensible questions almost immediately afterwards.

Website management

Nearly every company or organisation has its own website. Today, for most people, it is the first point of contact. Properly done, it should be a mine of information. It should be user-friendly and sufficiently well designed for the customer to navigate around the various pages quickly and easily. The corporate communicator is unlikely to have time to work on it. However, he should ensure that it is kept up-to-date and that when he navigates his way around it, he is not frustrated by lengthy downloads and information of which the latest is two years old. Companies are increasingly finding that a well managed website can attract favourable public reaction from its audiences. The corporate communicator should be in close liaison with the company's webmaster in order to maintain a quality website. The management, development and design of websites is a subject by itself, but your corporate communicator must be involved.

Letter writing to newspapers and magazines

Companies should not consider letter writing to be a reactive activity. Certainly any company, no matter its size, will attract letters from customers, satisfied and dissatisfied, shareholders and others who may have comments to make on a range of the company's activities. Your corporate communicator will be best positioned to draft replies and even send them out on the company's behalf. However, other opportunities will present themselves and your corporate communicator should find them whilst looking through his local newspapers. He should exploit the newspapers' wishes to carry letters from the public on matters of topical interest, anything from the changes to business rates, by-passes, local industry grants, employment, etc. After all, local industry probably accounts for the majority of the newspaper's readers and they buy the paper for local news. Letters from local companies will help meet the demand for local news from the readers.

The basic guidelines for letter writing are that the letters have to be:

- topical;

- in the style and length the paper prefers. If the letter doesn't need editing, it becomes much more attractive to the letter's editor;

- brief, lucid and to the point;

- exclusive to the newspaper.

Media relations

Media relations covers probably the most important part of any corporate communicator's work. If any company wants to be well regarded by its target audiences, it should aim to attract favourable press coverage to which the audience responds positively to the reports on a company's activities. Writing press releases is one part of media relations, other parts include:

- Press facilities
- Press briefings
- Press conferences
- Being the company spokesman

Chapter 12
Choosing a PR consultancy

If you think that the PR work, outlined in the previous chapter, is too much for your in-house corporate communicator to do part-time, but you feel you cannot justify a full time PR adviser, then think of using a PR consultancy. Choosing a PR consultancy is similar to choosing your auditors, your lawyers or your financial advisers.

Firstly, see if any of your staff can do PR. If you are going to limit yourself to simple local media relations, then a good writer with contacts in the local media may well be able to do it in-house. If the demand for PR then grows, you will have to decide if it is worth hiring your own full-time PR manager or a consultancy. A PR manager will cost you, all in, about £25,000. For the same amount or less, you could hire a consultancy without all the social service costs and draw on its collective experience and skills.

If you do decide to hire a consultancy, then ask a few questions and canvass opinion from other business colleagues about potentially suitable PR consultancies. Do they have a good track record in their specialised field, do they have satisfied clients, and do they deliver the desired results? Always talk to others who have been or are clients of the firm. If you start to hear some good testimonials of their efficiency and achievements, then it is probably worth making contact.

If you do not know anyone who has used or experienced a PR consultancy, then contact the Institute of Public Relations or the Public Relations Consultants Association. At the latest count, there are 7,000 members of the Institute of Public Relations. Tell them what you need and whether the location is important. They will provide you with a list of consultancies or individual freelance consultants who should largely meet with your requirements. Make contact with them by letter or email. Sometimes it is useful to have your consultancy in the neighbourhood, but in today's IT age, the Internet, emails and ease of travel often makes location unimportant. One of the most successful relationships I know is of a major environmental company in London who has used the same PR consultancy based in Guisborough, North Yorkshire, for over ten years.

So let's remind ourselves of the five Ws - Who, Why, What, When and Where. Then use them to identify your needs.

Why?	Why do you need a PT consultancy? Do you want to raise your profile? Do you need better internal communications? Do you need better communications with your suppliers, clients, local politicians or investors?
Who?	Who are your target audiences?
What?	What do you want the consultancy to do? Provide support for your marketing? Keep your target audiences informed? Create a corporate brand? Advise on lobbying,? Advise and execute your financial PR? What are the key messages and themes you want to send to your target audiences?
When?	When do you need these messages to be communicated to your target audiences? Is it to support an exhibition, a product launch, an application for planning permission or is it to announce the results of some new research and development?
Where?	Where are your chosen channels of communication? Are they individual letters, brochures, news releases in the trade and technical newspapers, a video or website?

The brief

Even if you have a choice of only one consultancy, write a brief, outlining what you want it to do for you and include a budget. Make sure the five Ws are included, define the nominated point of contact within the company, regularity of meetings, formal notes of meetings (normally called contact reports), limits on expenses, etc. The covering letter about the brief should invite the consultancies to phone or call in to discuss any points in the brief which need clarification and you or your nominated point of contact must be prepared to answer their questions accurately and objectively.

A good local consultancy in a small city will expect to charge about £500 a day, so a £15,000 budget will give you about 30 days a year. Big city consultancies will probably start at £750 a day. However, you should be able to take advantage of the fact that the larger the contract fee, the lower the daily rate, giving you more days for your fees.

To give you an idea of time management, a press release takes about one day to produce, i.e. to be briefed on the subject, producing the first draft, clearing it with the client, making the amendments, organising the distribution list, and then distributing it to the recipients. All the recipients will want their press release in different formats - by fax, by post or by email. A press visit or arranging press facilities will take about three days to organise and regular monthly meetings will take about half a day each.

Whatever is the final fee, you will have to pay the expenses incurred by the consultancy on your behalf, normally at cost and these include postage, telephone bills, travel, photocopying, incidental subsistence, etc. Your consultancy might also produce the printing for you or other major items of expenditure. These should be confirmed by means of a purchase order. If the consultancy pays for them on your behalf, then they may well charge a handling fee of say 17.5% to cover bad debts, etc. If you wish to avoid this handling charge, then offer to pay the consultancy in advance.

The choice

Once you have identified a number of consultancies which appear to fit the bill, you should then ask no more than three to make a full presentation. If you are spoilt for choice, you could invite, say, six of them to submit an outline PR programme that meets the brief, with a covering letter saying that the best three will be asked to make a full presentation.

An SME (small to medium enterprise) may well be a listed company and, if your company is, then it is well worth inviting consultancies who are capable of including financial PR in their programme.

If you are really unsure of which one to choose, then ask a PR consultant to advise you and perhaps help you select the short list for presentation. You may well want the consultant to sit in on the presentations.

When you invite the short listed consultancies to make their presentations, give them about 20 minutes to set up and then a clear time (say 60-90 minutes) for their presentations.

When the team comes in to make their presentation, there really should be no more than four and three is a preferable maximum. Initially you should be looking for WYSIWYG ('what you see is what you get'). The complete team should be the team that will be dedicated to servicing your requirements. Be prepared to be impressed by the team that is led by an Account Director and two Account Executives. They really will be the ones doing the work. If a main Board Director attends, then that director's input into servicing the account will be fairly minimal and you should think of that person as an overhead paid for by you. At the other end of the scale, beware of the consultancy that includes a graduate trainee in the team, as your fee will probably subsidise the graduate's training. Graduate trainees are vital to the development of any consultancy, but they really should not be put on display until they can be presented as trained Account Executives.

At the beginning, each member of the team should introduce themselves, their relevant experience and qualifications. The team leader should then present their credentials and outline their proposed programme in a fairly routine manner. However, do look to see just how well they make the presentation. Has it been well rehearsed? Is the handout material to support the presentation well laid out? Does the team look confident?

A well rehearsed presentation will fit neatly into the allocated period with time for questions and you will not feel rushed. They probably will have some empathy with you and it will show.

At the end of the presentations you will have to be coldly dispassionate. One team may look smart and savvy but can they really deliver better than the others? One effective method to prevent you being blinded by smart, smooth teams is to start with a matrix of the points which are absolutely essential to you and discuss each one and award each consultancy an appropriate tick or cross:

	Cons 1	Cons 2	Cons 3
Credentials	✓	✗	✓
Team experience & qualifications	✗	✓	✗
Track record	✓	✓	✓
Financial PR	✓	✗	✓
Crisis management	✗	✓	✗
Media relations	✓	✓	✓

Costs	✗	✓	✓
Ideas	✓	✓	✗
Location	✗	✓	✓
Resources	✓	✗	✓

A subsidiary in a company I was with had invited in four consultancies to make presentations. Afterwards, we identified 14 points which had to be discussed. A matrix, similar to the one above, was drawn on a flip chart. There were two large consultancies and two small ones. The two large consultancies only had eight ticks each and the two small ones had 12 ticks each, albeit their crosses were different. Being present as PR adviser, I told the divisional MD that as they were virtually equal, it was now a matter of personal chemistry and it was up to him and his team to decide with which they would prefer to work. When you have made your choice based on the number of positive points which meet your company's needs, do consider the personal chemistry. If they are any good, they will be living in your pockets for some time and there must be mutual respect between you and them. So do look at the team before you finally decide and ask yourself whether your company and you can do business with them.

The follow-up

Each consultancy must be immediately sent a letter thanking them for their presentation and in the majority of the cases regretting that they will not be granted the contract this time. The winning consultancy must be invited around to finalise the details of the contract. The Institute of Public Relations has a good draft contract on its website which should provide you with the basis of your contract. Make sure the contract defines the fee, the notice period, expenses, project cost limitations, period of notice and, most importantly, the programme of work to be carried out.

When they start working for you, the sign that a consultancy is probably good is that they phone you more than you phone them. They should be a powerhouse of ideas, initiative and advice based on the up-to-date information they gain from you during their regular contacts and meetings.

The contact details for the Institute of Public Relations are as follows:

The Old Trading House, 15 Northburgh Street, London, EC1V 0PR. Tel: 020 7253 5151; Fax: 020 7490 0588; Email: info@pr.org.uk

Chapter 13

Lobbying
Communicating with politicians

What you'll find in this chapter:

➡ Corresponding with MPs
➡ Ministerial contact
➡ The legislative process

Lobbying has connotations ranging from the decidedly dodgy to the remarkably respectable. The communications between politicians and the public is two-way. When the public talk to politicians it's lobbying; when politicians talk to the public it's known as attracting support. It's a symbiotic relationship. If we are prepared to be influenced by politicians, then we should be aware that they are dependent on our votes to put them into or out of office. So why do politicians adjust their manifestos? Why do they put emphasis on various parts of the manifesto in times of potential trouble? Very simply, because they want to gain your support, because they believe, in varying degrees of confidence, that they know what the electorate wants.

Why and how do they perceive any changes in public support? Well, obviously, they conduct public opinion polls to assess what is foremost in the public's mind. But how do they know what to look for? Well, there is a two-way communication between the politicians and the public which occurs through various methods: letters to politicians, constituency surgeries, lobbying and public meetings.

For all elected representatives, industry is vital in their constituency or ward. Without it, there would be no employment and it would be a deprived area with all the associated problems. An area with a good diverse industrial base supports not just those directly employed in industry, but also the shops, garages, employment agencies, professional services, pubs and restaurants. If an area is dependent on one industry, then the area will stand or fall on its success or failure. For example, on the outskirts of Reading at Arborfield, there is a major Army base that naturally supports a large number of local businesses. A regiment based there was posted to Bosnia for a six-month tour of duty and whilst it was away, more than half the businesses in the area closed down. The locality's source of income just temporarily disappeared. This is perhaps an extreme example of an area dependent on just one industry, but it gives an indication why local politicians much prefer a diverse commercial and industrial base for the area's economic well-being.

Corresponding with MPs

The vast majority of businesses and organisations tend to be more influenced by local government decisions regarding planning permissions, business rates, parking, access, etc. If a business is to protect its own interests, it must not neglect to maintain contact with politicians at all the necessary levels. Politicians attract a great deal of media interest and their main topic of debate will be constituency matters, which will include the business and industry sectors. Liaising with your MP will ensure that he is well informed and promoting issues important to your organisation.

Getting in touch just once a year will make no impact on a politician; only those organisations that keep in contact regularly succeed. The methods of communication can vary, from inviting the politician to meet you and the workforce at the factory, to a meeting at his surgery, in the town hall, at constituency social events or even in the House of Commons. You might even keep in contact by mail or even email.

When you are informing a politician, keep it brief. Any letter should be kept to one sheet of paper, with three or four paragraphs. They have more than enough mail to digest, and the simple, self-contained letters are always appreciated.

When I worked for a regulated industry, the company sent out its annual reports and accounts and its financial results to all the MPs in its area. These reports were sent out with a covering letter, which stated that the MP might like to read it.

Assuming that MPs would be reluctant to read an annual report or set of financial results, I instead drafted a letter on behalf of my Chief Executive, which, in two paragraphs, stated that the company had increased turnover, improved dividends and provided an even better level of service and prices for the consumers in the politician's constituency. The Chief Executive signed the letter and it was posted to the MPs with a copy of the annual report.

Much to the Chief Executive's surprise and delight he received six replies saying that they were pleased that the company was looking after their constituents so well. It was the first time he had had any acknowledgements and what had made it successful was that the letter had summarised the annual report and added the extra spin on improved levels of services for the constituents.

When VIPs visit your factory or exhibition stand, it is much better to have an action shot by a distinctive company product than the stiff formal group picture. Catching the Chairman of Rolls-Royce, Sir Ralph Robins, as he animatedly briefs the Prime Minister at the company's stand at the Farnborough Air Show resulted in a more interesting and useable photograph.

Ministerial contact

You can also maintain effective communication with Ministers, the councillors who chair the various council departments and the EU Commissioners. Most businessmen think it's best to write directly to them, should you have a question which needs clarification or perhaps you have a criticism. Your letter will go to the department's correspondence section and you will normally receive a reply within about ten working days. It will be signed by an official but, under normal circumstances, will probably not satisfy you.

Instead it is much more effective to write to your MP, MEP (Member of European Parliament) or councillor making your point or question and asking if they can contact the relevant Minister. Any such letter from an MP or MEP goes straight to the Minister's Private Office. From there, one of the Assistant Private Secretaries (normally a high-flying civil servant) will forward it to the head of the relevant division requesting a draft answer for signature by the Minister within a few days. The Minister replies to all letters from MPs and MEPs personally and as such the Minister takes a personal interest in the letter and in the reply.

You may want a meeting with a Minister to discuss points relevant to your business. To be effective, this must be a two-pronged approach. First of all, make contact with the relevant official in the department and make sure he is properly briefed on the subject. Next, use your local MP, MEP or councillor to support your request for a meeting. When the meeting happens, do invite your MP to accompany you. Meanwhile, in the Minister's Private Office, your meeting will be scheduled and departmental officials will be asked to produce a ministerial briefing note prior to the meeting. So when you have your meeting, the Minister will have been properly briefed and will have on outline of the options open to him. As a result, he will be better able to support your request and be more supportive of you because you gave his officials briefing material beforehand.

When I worked in the defence industry, one of the company's divisional MDs managed to arrange a meeting with the Minister of Defence Procurement. The meeting lasted 30 minutes and the MD did virtually all the talking. When he came out he was seriously disappointed. He said the Minister just sat there stony-faced, said very little and promised nothing. I asked the MD if he had provided any briefing material to the relevant official on the subject for the meeting and he said he had not. As there had been no pre-meeting briefing material, the Minister attended with virtually no idea of the subject of the meeting and therefore absolutely no idea what his reaction should be to the request from the MD.

In the House of Commons, MPs form all sorts of groups, regional groups, and industrial groups, so one can exploit some of these various groupings. If your MP is not sympathetic, for example, to your defence industry business, you can always contact members of the relevant committee, in this case, the members of the Defence Back Bench Committee. If you are really stuck on whom best to contact, then surprisingly your MP, MEP or councillor is probably the best to ask. Usually they will be pleased to help. After all, they are there to use their influence.

The legislative process

All Parliamentary legislation, Acts of Parliament and Orders in Council go through a process of public consultation. An Act of Parliament starts life as a Bill, followed by White Papers, Green Papers, three readings and a committee stage in both Houses of Parliament before receiving Royal Assent and becoming law. Orders in Council provide the government with the opportunity to introduce into law some legislation with some considerable speed. Sometimes this can be done in as little as a day and when this happens, it normally is to do with security matters.

For the average businessman, normal perusal of the daily papers should give you an indication of what legislation is likely to affect business and the public, political and commercial reaction to it. At this stage, if the Bill looks as if it might impact on your business, acquire a copy of the Green Paper and check for likely effects on your business. If there are consequences for your business, write to the relevant official outlining your objections (or even support) for the Bill. These are taken seriously as the Parliamentary draughtsmen are not always fully *au fait* on the minutiae of business and a correction made at this time can save much embarrassment and time later. It is well worth sending a copy of your representation to your local MP with a covering letter. Should your representation not work, then you have the option to write to your MP and ask for his support, making sure that the local implications of the legislation is well highlighted, viz, jobs at risk, threat to inward investment, unwanted burdensome overheads, threats to exports, etc. All of these are the sorts of issues which MPs know will help them to be seen as good local MPs and aid them in gaining votes at the next election. They will also highlight this assistance to their constituents in the local media.

Under normal circumstances this approach has a good chance of success. If not, then it is worthwhile linking in with your local Chamber of Commerce or regional office of the Confederation of British Industry to do some collective lobbying with companies who are likely to find themselves equally inconvenienced by this legislation.

Influencing legislation at both local government and EU level should be initially taken using your local councillor or MEP as a means of supporting your case.

Chapter 14
Crisis management

What you'll find in this chapter:

⟼   Crisis management guidelines
⟼   Pre-planned contingency package checklist
⟼   Preparing the company spokesperson

Descended from the apes? My dear, we hope that it is not true. But if it is, let us pray that it may not become generally known.

Wife of a Canon of Worcester Cathedral

Nearly every company will have to face crisis management at some time or another. Be it a customer being badly injured on your site, customers' problems using your products, fire, fraud, faulty products, product recall, etc. To do full justice to this subject is a book in itself, but here are some guidelines as to what a manager must do to handle the media in a crisis:

- Be in control

- Marshall your thoughts and information

- Prepare your statement

- Prepare your questions-and-answers brief

- Identify the key bullet points

- Co-ordinate within the company

- Meet the press

- Report back

1. Introduction

How ready are you to meet the media challenge if you and your company hit the wrong headlines today? Without a pre-planned and rehearsed contingency package, known by everyone, a crisis can quickly become a catastrophe.

2. Where to start

- Analyse and prepare for what could go wrong.

- Plan and prepare your counter-plan - adopt not the 'if' but the 'when' philosophy.

- Allow for the unforeseen.

3. Create a plan and communicate it internally

- Establish laid down procedures for dealing with any incident that could lead to adverse publicity.

- Ensure that the procedures are known and understood by everyone likely to be involved.

4. Practice makes perfect

- Time spent on rehearsals is never wasted.

- Identify skill shortages and implement the appropriate training: media interview techniques, preparing the company spokesperson(s) and how to face the public.

5. Managing the public perception

- Adopt the right attitude.

- Be honest, open and positive.

6. When under siege from the media

- It is vital that you communicate with the outside world.

- Put your key messages across.

- Have your prepared question-and-answer brief updated to deal with specific situations.

- Establish the precise facts.

- Decide what should be said and what should not be said.

- Decide when it should be said and how.

- Establish an agreed press line and company statement, putting events into perspective and highlighting any positive aspects, for use by all.

- Make sure your website is kept right up-to-date, as it will be an excellent channel of communication with your target audiences.

- Pre-identify and train the company spokesperson(s).

- All levels must communicate the same message(s).

- Keep your PR staff fully informed.

- Do not let the press take the initiative by THEM telling YOU that you have a problem.

- Do not be naive and assume that 'it will not get out'.

- Ensure that all levels in the company have the press line, Q&A brief and the company statement, as soon as possible.

- Beware of the press playing one source off against another.

- Have laid-down procedures for dealing with media enquiries out of office hours.

- Speed and accuracy are essential. Journalists have deadlines that have to be met. If you do not give them the facts, they will speculate and invariably get it wrong.

- Unless you already have the company media package - the press line, the statement and the Q&A brief - take any press enquiries and say you will return the call as soon as possible. Try to call back within half-an-hour, even if it is only to say that you do not have the answer.

- A good truthful reason must be given for not providing a full answer, such as 'a man has been charged with a criminal offence and the matter is now sub-judice'.

- Security may be given when it is a genuine reason for not answering, but it never should be used as a cover-up excuse.

- Under no circumstances must attempts be made to mislead the media with a cover story; your organisation's credibility is sacrosanct.

- A 'no comment' will merely reinforce the allegations in the media's mind. If you refuse to co-operate, you only have yourself to blame if an unbalanced or inaccurate story is published or broadcast.

- If an article or report is incorrect or misleading, you may like to obtain a correction, ideally with another story, in order to put the matter right.

- Take care with the release of casualty information until you are sure that the next of kin have been informed. Normally the police will release this information as a matter of course once they know that the next of kin have been told.

7. The importance of employee communications

- It is a common error, unintentionally or deliberately, not to inform employees.

- Dangerous consequences of rumour and leaks to the media will make the situation worse.

- Employee communications must be timely and accurate.

8. Summary

The level of success in achieving positive public perception will be determined by the existence of a contingency plan, already in place within an organisation, that can be put into action promptly by a crisis management team with identified and trained resources, and also by how the company responds to the media.

Checklist of points to be considered in a pre-planned contingency package

1. Types of emergency

- Terrorism
- Serious crime
- Security breach
- Accident
- Corporate crisis (e.g. hostile takeover attempt)
- Environmental disaster/pollution
- Sabotage (of equipment, food, drink, etc)

2. Levels of emergency

- Limited impact
- Serious incident
- Major incident

3. Lines of communication

- Initial call-outs
- Mobilising management and/or head office staff
- Informing consultants/agents/legal advisers
- Levels of authority
- Liaison with other interested parties (e.g. government ministries, police, government inspectors, etc)

4. *Departmental roles*

- Chief Executive/Country Manager
- Administrator
- PR /press office
- Company webmaster
- Security department
- Legal adviser
- Company secretary
- Spokesperson(s)
- Logistic and material control
- Chief accountant/banks

5. *Additional resources*

- Police
- Local authorities
- Government ministries and agencies

6. *Logistics*

- Hotel accommodation
- Couriers - bikes, taxis, cars, helicopters
- Next of kin
- Funds and finance
- Communications
- Catering

7. *Incident Press Office (IPO)*

- Role
- Location
- Authorisation to establish
- Staffing
- Call-out
- Communications (phones, fax, email, Internet access, etc)
- Control and management
- Press line, statement, Q&A brief
- Press facilities and policy
- Involvement of police authorities
- Next of kin notification
- Interface with the corporate head office

8. *Types of caller*

- The media
- The public
- Investors
- Government ministries and agencies
- Local authorities
- Pressure groups
- Cranks/hoaxers
- Trade unions and labour organisations

9. Co-ordination

- Police
- Government ministries and agencies
- Local authorities
- Social services
- Welfare agencies

10. Call-out box

- Purpose
- Contents
- Authorised holders
- Accessibility

11. Miscellaneous

- Telephone logs
- Confidential telephone lists
- Yellow pages
- Transcripts from the broadcast media
- Maps
- Media lists
- Background and briefing notes, including corporate literature and videos
- Pre-dated authorisations
- Media security passes
- Next of kin routines

'Daddy! We video'd this really boring man being interviewed on TV - and guess what? He looked just like you!'

Preparing the company spokesperson

1. Decide in advance precisely what your message is and don't deviate from it.

2. Brief and rehearse your spokesperson. Try to spot the 'nasties' that may emerge, and remember to rehearse him with 'hostile' or 'loaded' questions too.

3. On the morning of the press conference or interview, discover if there are any new factors that may involve a change of emphasis or even a change in the spokespersons personal position or situation. You are also there to protect him.

4. Check whether the spokesperson is going to circulate among media guests after the press conference. That's when people are most vulnerable and frequently reveal something indiscreet. Remind your spokesperson that **nothing is ever 'off the record'**.

5. No alcohol for **anybody** until it is all over.

6. Establish the ground rules with the media. Ask them to identify themselves when they ask questions. Note their questions - an ideal opportunity to record (without being obvious about it) the questions and answers for future reference.

7. Take the spokesperson with you on a visit to the location of the press conference. Decide seating arrangements. Do check the background to where the spokesperson will be sitting as some photographs taken at odd angles can play havoc with company names or slogans.

8   Check the spokespersons clothes and the way he/she sits:

    *   flies open?
    *   cleavage?
    *   stockings?
    *   hair?
    *   dandruff?

9. Introduce the spokesperson with style and grace.

10. Be prepared to step in if things get out of control: you are the hosts; the media are your guests.

11. **Stay cool, calm and collected. You are in control so control it!**

Summary overview

What you'll find in this chapter:
▸ Media relations
▸ The media: friend and foe

Media relations

There are five main principles:

1. Take the initiative

Companies succeed by taking the initiative and conducting a proactive media relations policy. Companies should think of what they are doing well, what would be of interest to the press and then release the facts to the media. The easiest way is to generate press releases on your successes and appointments and invite the press in for visits, briefings, demonstrations, etc. If you develop a good track record with the media for presenting a flow of good stories, then your success rate will increase, and when disaster occurs, your friendly media are less likely to be hostile to you.

It is only possible to generate a continual flow of material for positive publicity if the directors, managers and others in companies and organisations keep their corporate communicator fully informed of matters of potential press interest, be they positive or adverse. It is probably more important to keep the corporate communicator informed of the adverse events. As a result, should he be ambushed by the press on such a subject, he will give a much more confident reaction to the press and, with luck, even be able to kill the story. Caught unawares and ignorant, the press will assume that the company has something to hide as even the corporate communicator has not been informed.

2. Have a media plan

When you are dealing with the media, you should think about what you would like to see in the press in the immediate future that supports your company or organisation's aim.

3. Be frank within the limits of commercial and personal confidentiality

Today's legislation defines the limits of what you can say to the press, because of the Data Protection Act, company law, libel laws, Stock Exchange regulations and commercial confidentiality. The one that is probably most likely to be broken is commercial confidentiality. People tend to be so delighted with a new order or a new development that they forget that with new orders you must have the agreement of the client before you can even think about making an announcement. You must also consider whether you might be giving away information to the competition. You should apply the same criteria if your client wants to publicise your part in their success.

4. Gain the confidence of the journalists

As the media is always working to tight deadlines, do give them an answer as soon as possible. Ask when their deadline is, and even if you cannot make the deadline, phone back to say that you cannot make it. They may not like it, but at least they know they have to run with what they have and perhaps you may have the answer for the next edition. However, do remember that if the newspaper has a report that is perhaps detrimental to your company or organisation, then a prompt and accurate reply can at least minimise the damage or even kill the story.

5. When the media ask questions, involve your corporate communicator

The more the corporate communicator and his Chief Executive can meet the press, be seen to be a credible source of news and have empathy with the journalists, the more the correspondent will have confidence in the company. Consequently, any reports he writes about the company will more than likely be positive. The corporate communicator should try to arrange a regular programme of lunches and other occasions where the Chief Executive and his managers can meet the press, but a good frequency is no more than four times per year.

The media: friend and foe

The media can easily be your friend or foe. By realising what a journalist does and the why and how of his modus operandi, you will have the media as your friend complete with the advantages of having a good conduit of communication to many of your target audiences. When dealing with the media, do remember the following points:

1. **Your credibility, as an individual and as a company, is sacrosanct.**

2. The media is not infallible.

3. You have no divine right to appear in newspapers, or on radio or TV.

4. The media is there to get a good story: give it to them.

5. If you can't provide the media with a good story, they'll find one anyway! So provide them with **maximum information**.

6. Remember that only the media decides what it publishes. Sometimes that may seem unfair, but that's the way it is.

7. Resist the temptation to be over-defensive and pedantic, but if something is published that is factually wrong, get a correction on the record. Many stories are written from material culled from the newspaper's library of press cuttings. Today this will also include press cuttings accessed from newspaper archives on the World Wide Web. Get **your** version, response, or correction into the cuttings too.

8. The media is anxious to get it right but some newspapers are not averse to being selective about the information they use: 'facts can spoil a good story'!

9. The media has no divine right to receive answers, but it has a perfect right to ask the questions.

10. If you don't know the answer, don't lie, guess or stall. Tell them you'll find out and call them back. But if you promise to do so, then **you must call back**!

11. Don't be drawn into speculation or giving a 'personal view, off the record' as that will lead to disaster.

12. Never say 'no comment' as it really does make it sound as if you have something to hide!

13. Get to know your regular journalists but be careful about generating favourites. There will be times when the close relationship you develop can be of mutual benefit. But favours can sometimes prove embarrassing too.

14. Never underestimate the knowledge and skill of journalists, particularly specialist correspondents. They have extraordinary access to industrial and political leaders and they can double-fault you very easily.

15. Always treat your local media with the same respect and openness you show towards the national media. They operate within the same community as your company and in many cases, they string for the national media.

16. Local media - newspapers, radio and TV - feed their respective networks. A story for the local radio or TV station may well hit the network. Even the 'Six O'Clock News' and 'News at Ten' are not averse to finding something 'different'.

17. Look for a 'social factor' you can inject into stories. Never underplay your importance in the community, your contribution to that community and your involvement in all aspects of that community.

18 Provide pictures - stills for newspapers, clips of film or video for TV. If you have already undertaken some 'specialist' filming under circumstances that can't easily be duplicated, then use it.

19. Everybody likes artists' impressions too but they must be well produced. The media will either use the impression you give them or adapt and draw their own. Television has a very exciting graphics capability now; information and impressions will help them get those graphics right, thereby enhance the quality of information they want to convey to the audience.

20. Never be afraid to offer stories. Suggest and encourage. If they take up the offer, then ease the path for the media team.

21. **Never be afraid of the media. They can be your finest allies. Treat them honestly, and please, never forget that it's your credibility that's always on the line!**

Index

More books available from Law Pack...

How to Make Money Online

Forget the high-profile dot com failures - there are businesses out there making money online. This guide includes what will and won't sell, how to avoid e-business mistakes, how to give website visitors the confidence to buy online, getting payments, security software and systems, digital certificates and e-signatures, selling advertising space, supplying content, and much more!

Code B604	ISBN 1 902646 76 2	PB	
250 x 199mm	160pp	£9.99	Jan 2002

Online Marketing Strategies

What are your goals for your website? Is your website marketing you, or are you marketing it? And how will your website relate to your business's overall marketing strategy? This book provides guidance on building marketing into your website, on monitoring, evaluating and improving your internet or extranet site and on coordinating online and offline marketing strategies.

Code B602	ISBN 1 902646 75 4	PB	
250 x 199mm	160pp	£9.99	Dec 2001

Secrets of Successful Websites

Some websites get it right, many get it wrong. This guide divulges what makes a successful site. It covers identifying the audience and their needs, choosing the right model for your site, choosing the right technology and ISP, getting the best help with implementation, design and branding, risk management and testing procedures.

Code B601	ISBN 1 902646 74 6	PB	
250 x 199mm	160pp	£9.99	Dec 2001

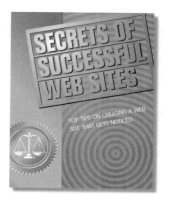

To order, visit www.lawpack.co.uk or call 020 7394 4040

More books available from Law Pack...

Legal Advice Handbook

Where do you go for legal advice? As the sources of both free and paid-for legal advice become more diverse and specific areas of law demand greater specialisation from the advice givers, the need for a consumer guide to this expanding, unmapped network has never been greater. Solicitor Tessa Shepperson has gathered together extensive research data and produced an invaluable handbook.

Code B427	ISBN 1 902646 71 1	PB	
A5	130pp	£7.99	October 2001

How to Complain Effectively

Faulty goods, shoddy service, poor advice... these are things most of us, at some time, feel we have good reason to complain about. In this practical guide, Steve Wiseman draws on his extensive experience as a Citizens Advice Bureau manager and tells you how to ensure your complaint has maximum impact, whether it be against your local shop or a government department.

Code B430	ISBN 1 902646 80 0	PB	
A5	160pp	£7.99	May 2001

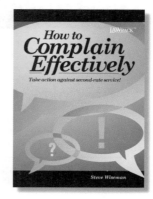

Tax Answers at a Glance

With the emphasis on self-assessment, we all need to have a hold of the panoply of taxes now levied by government. Compiled by tax experts and presented in question-and- answer format, this handy guide provides a useful summary of income tax, VAT, capital gains, inheritance, pensions, self-employment, partnerships, land and property, trusts and estates, corporation tax, stamp duty and more.

Code B425	ISBN 1 902646 62 2	PB	
A5	130pp	£7.99	April 2001

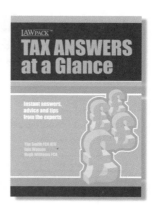

To order, visit www.lawpack.co.uk or call 020 7394 4040

More books available from Law Pack...

Company Minutes & Resolutions

Company Minutes & Resolutions Made Easy is what every busy company secretary or record-keeper needs. Maintaining good, up-to-date records is not only sensible business practice, but also a legal requirement of Companies House. This Made Easy Guide makes the whole process straightforward. It provides an invaluable source of essential documents that no company should be without.

Code B501	ISBN 1 902646 41 X	PB	
250 x 199mm	190pp	£9.99	1st edition

Debt Collection

Chasing debts is a pain which all businesses can do without. Unfortunately, unpaid bills are an all-too frequent problem for business owners and managers. Debt Collection Made Easy helps you solve it. It provides expert advice and tips on resolving disputes, reducing the risks of bad debt, getting money out of reluctant payers, letter cycles, credit insurance, export credit, and much more.

Code B512	ISBN 1 902646 42 8	PB	
250 x 199mm	134pp	£9.99	1st edition

Employment Law

Written by an employment law solicitor, Employment Law Made Easy is a comprehensive, reader-friendly source of reference which will provide answers to practically all your employment law questions. Essential knowledge for employers and employees!

Code B502	ISBN 1 904053 08 4	PB	
250 x 199mm	176pp	£9.99	3rd edition

To order, visit www.lawpack.co.uk or call 020 7394 4040

More books available from Law Pack...

Limited Company Formation

Incorporation as a limited liability company is the preferred structure for thousands of successful businesses. *Limited Company Formation Made Easy* Guide explains why, and shows you how to set up your own limited liability company easily and inexpensively. It provides detailed but easy to follow instructions, background information, completed examples of Companies House forms and drafts of other necessary documents.

Code B503	ISBN 1 902646 43 6	PB
250 x 199mm	112pp	£9.99	1st edition

Profitable Mail-Order

Mail-order business is big business, and it's growing year by year. Setting up and running your own mail-order business can be fun as well as profitable. This *Made Easy* Guide shows you how to do it, explaining the vital importance of product profile, building valuable mailing lists, effective advertising and a whole lot more. It divulges the mail-order secrets that ensure success!

Code B510	ISBN 1 902646 46 0	PB
250 x 199mm	206pp	£9.99	1st edition

Running Your Own Business

You have a business idea that you want to put into action, but you also want advice on the realities of setting up and running a business: this *Made Easy* Guide is for you. It takes you through the business-creation process, from assessing your aptitude and ideas, to funding and business plans.

Code B511	ISBN 1 902646 47 9	PB
250 x 199mm	140pp	£9.99	1st edition

To order, visit www.lawpack.co.uk or call 020 7394 4040